Prentice Hall Series
in Advanced Business Communication

Guide to

Managerial Persuasion and Influence

Jane Thomas
University of Michigan Business School

Mary Munter
Series Editor

PEARSON
Prentice
Hall

Upper Saddle River, New Jersey 07458

Library of Congress Cataloging-in-Publication Data

Thomas, Jane.
   Guide to managerial persuasion and influence / Jane Thomas.
      p. cm.—(Prentice Hall series in advanced communication)
   Includes bibliographical references and index.
   ISBN 0-13-140568-3 (pbk. : alk. paper)
      1. Communication in management. 2. Persuasion (Rhetoric) I. Title. II. Series.

HD30.3.T459 2003
658.4´5—dc21   2003046386

Acquisitions Editor: David Parker
Editor-in-Chief: Jeff Shelstad
Assistant Editor: Ashley Keim
Editorial Assistant: Melissa Yu
Executive Marketing Manager: Shannon Moore
Marketing Assistant: Patrick Danzuso
Senior Managing Editor (Production): Judy Leale
Production Assistant: Joseph DeProspero
Associate Director, Manufacturing: Vincent Scelta
Production Manager: Arnold Vila
Manufacturing Buyer: Diane Peirano
Cover Design: Kiwi Design
Cover Illustration/Photo: Kiwi Design
Composition/Full-Service Project Management: Rainbow Graphics/Linda Begley
Printer/Binder: Phoenix

Credits and acknowledgments borrowed from other sources and reproduced, with permission, in this textbook appear on appropriate page within text.

Pearson Education LTD.
Pearson Education Singapore, Pte. Ltd
Pearson Education, Canada, Ltd
Pearson Education–Japan

Pearson Education Australia PTY, Limited
Pearson Education North Asia Ltd
Pearson Educación de Mexico, S.A. de C.V.
Pearson Education Malaysia, Pte. Ltd

10 9 8 7
ISBN 0-13-140568-3

Contents

CHAPTER IV

CHAPTER V

CHAPTER VI

Preface

HOW THIS BOOK CAN HELP YOU

If your business success depends on your ability to persuade and influence others, this book can help you. In it, you will find specific advice on how to:

- Appeal to and motivate different kinds of people
- Enhance your credibility
- Develop your working relationships
- Be influential within your organizational hierarchy
- Gain compliance and agreement with your ideas
- Influence superiors, subordinates, and customers
- Make your points logically
- Persuade in different organizational or country cultures

WHO CAN USE THIS BOOK

This book will be useful to you if your ability to get things done depends on dealing with other people through persuasive communication skills. Consider the following:

- Almost all of your communication at work has a persuasive component.
- The more responsibility you acquire, the more you must deal with others to get your work done.
- Being persuasive at work depends on developing and maintaining relationships.

WHY THIS BOOK WAS WRITTEN

Many of the MBA students and executives I have taught have told me that they want a quick, readable guide to the issues discussed in class. In developing this course, I discovered that most books on persuasion are long, tedious, and academic. This book, in contrast, is brief, relevant, and reader-friendly.

- *Brief:* This is a summary of key ideas that does not include lengthy academic explanations, cases, or exercises.
- *Relevant:* Only the relevant issues are included, issues you can use immediately in your work. You will not find digressions or full explanations of the underlying theories that support the advice presented.
- *Reader-friendly:* I have tried to make the format easy and quick to read, with charts and headings that should help you to skim the information.

HOW THIS BOOK IS ORGANIZED

This book is organized into six chapters.

I. Develop Your Argument. To help you construct a supportable argument for a position or decision you have made, you will learn how to state your position clearly, provide reasons that support your position, choose evidence that supports your reasons, and make them all fit together logically.

II. Check Your Logic. In this chapter you will learn strategies for creating a logical message structure as well as for avoiding the pitfalls of unfair and illogical arguments.

III. Analyze Your Audience. This chapter provides a number of ways to analyze your particular audience. The chapter includes questions to ask yourself as well as a number of approaches to gaining information about your audience.

IV. Motivate Your Audience. Two important aspects of persuasion—audience motivation techniques and credibility enhancement techniques—are covered in this chapter.

V. Study the Organization. In this chapter, you will learn how to analyze organizational structures and ways of sharing information—as well as your own position in the organization, based on the relationships involved and your credibility.

VI. Consider the Culture. Information on differences among the various world cultures is provided in this chapter, which addresses such issues as context, time, view of society, view of employee, view of authority, silence, and gender. You will find advice and strategies for dealing with people from cultures other than your own.

ACKNOWLEDGMENTS

This book would not have been written without the encouragement and support of many people. First of all, I offer my profound gratitude to Priscilla Rogers—my friend, colleague, mentor, and chief motivator for almost everything I do. I am also grateful to my other University of Michigan colleagues Anne Harrington and Nancy Kotzian. Their advice, conversations, and knowledge shared with me over the years have helped me to think, teach, and write in the exciting and challenging Michigan environment.

To Mary Munter, editor of this series, I offer my sincere thanks for all her work, advice, suggestions, and insistence on excellence; I believe this book is much more readable and relevant because of her contributions. I am also grateful to my colleagues at the Association for Business Communication, who are among the best, most supportive colleagues of any academic association in the world. Finally, I want to acknowledge my sources in the bibliography.

Special thanks go to Hugh, David, Hugh Jr., Clay, and Bessy, who always think my abilities are greater than they actually are.

Jane Thomas
University of Michigan
Business School

Introduction

HOW IS MANAGERIAL PERSUASION DIFFERENT?

If you are a business person, you spend most of your workdays making decisions and recommendations and then persuading superiors, peers, subordinates, and customers that your decisions are good ones. This kind of persuasion is much different from persuasion for a mass audience (advertising), persuasion for large groups (motivational speaking and writing), or persuasion dealing strictly with sales (collection letters or sales information).

Business people do sell—they sell themselves and their ideas—but they do this most successfully when they are able to work through their established relationships. This book deals with ways to persuade others by taking into account the organizational environment. It also shows you ways to develop and maintain influence in professional relationships. This kind of persuasion is based on a wide range of situations and on continually developing relationships. It takes place within an organizational hierarchy and has different objectives. These characteristics are discussed below. Specifically, managerial persuasion . . .

1. Is based on a wide range of situations

Your work as a businessperson consists to a large degree of communicating: face-to-face in private or public meetings, on the telephone, through videoconferencing, by email, or through other written communication channels. Consider the following schedule of a typical manager:

SCHEDULE FOR MONDAY, MARCH 14		
Time	**Person**	**Reason**
7:30 A.M.	Andrea—meet for breakfast	• Urge her to deal quickly with the problem with Jasper before we get a lawsuit.
8:30 A.M.	Conference call with Jones at EPA	• Discuss environmental problem; we're doing all we can.
9:00 A.M.	Work on Manager's Message for Annual Report	• Legal issues in Manager's Message.
11:00 A.M.	Jack—meeting	• Talk over Manager's Message; need his signature by end of day.
12:30 P.M.	Rob—lunch	
2:00 P.M.	Acct. dept. manager	• Explain why we can't do flextime right now.
3:00 P.M.	Work on presentation for Thursday night's board meeting	
5:00 P.M.	Rob—meet	• Get signature on message!
7:00 P.M.	Work on board presentation	

This manager's entire day consisted of writing and speaking on a variety of issues, each of which involved persuasion based on personal relationships with superiors, peers, and subordinates within her organizational hierarchy.

2. Is based on personal relationships

As the previous example demonstrates, you know your audience in your workplace personally. You will know some people better than others, but since most of your communication is in regard to the operation of some part of the organization, most of the people you communicate with are known entities.

Analyzing interpersonal relationships with audience: Before you begin any actual persuasive communication, you will need to bear in mind who will receive your message. Will your audience consist of one person or many? Will you have to educate your audience on the facts of the issue? What is your audience's place in the organization and is this position above, below, or equal to you? Is your audience a part of an outside organization, and if so, what is your relationship and relative status? Does your audience agree with your position? What special expectations might your audience have? These questions can help you tailor your message when making communication choices and building on the influence you have built up over time with this audience. We will expand on these issues and discuss audience analysis in depth in Chapter III.

3. Takes place within an organizational hierarchy

An organization's culture, whether it is yours or an outside organization, will determine to a large extent how your relationships are expressed. To persuade effectively in organizational cultures, you will need to take into account the level of hierarchy, the level of centralization, and the level of job specialization. These issues are covered in depth in Chapter V and are briefly summarized below as part of determining the organizational culture.

Determining the culture: Several factors provide clues about an organization's culture and communication practices. Some of these factors are clear to any observer; however, many of them must be discovered by close observation over time. The questions below are guidelines:

- *Level of hierarchy:* Are the reporting relationships firmly established and enforced?
- *Level of centralization:* To what degree can decisions be made by lower-ranking employees?
- *Level of job specialization:* Are job responsibilities clear and finite or do jobs and functions often flow together?

The following chart provides an overview of organizational culture and its effect on communication.

COMMUNICATION IMPLICATIONS OF ORGANIZATIONAL CULTURE		
	Strong	**Weak**
Hierarchy	• Chain of command must be followed. • A superior position provides organizational power.	• Chain of command may not be clear or may be bypassed. • Organizational power is not automatically provided by superior position.
Centralization	• Top managers make most decisions that matter. • Decisions, once made, are difficult to change.	• Decision maker may be closer in rank and better known by communicator. • Identifying decision maker can sometimes be difficult.
Specialization	• Jobs are highly specialized. • Understanding job limits is essential in order to achieve objectives.	• Responsibilities and functions can flow into other's job areas. • Identifying appropriate audience can be difficult.

You will notice that most of the characteristics become clear over time, but a perceptive person will learn about the culture through attention to communication practices. The traditional U.S. company is strong in terms of hierarchy, centralization, and specialization. However, new industries, such as technology-sector organizations, and the growth of globalization have changed many organizational cultures from strongly hierarchical to flatter and less centralized. You can find more complete coverage on organizational issues in Chapter V.

Establishing credibility: The factors in an organization's culture discussed above not only affect communication but also have an impact on your credibility, as covered in Chapter IV. The following factors influence credibility:

- *Rank:* (1) highly influential in hierarchical, centralized, or specialized cultures; (2) less influential in democratic, decentralized, or unspecialized cultures

- *Perceived expertise:* (1) helpful if you have knowledge in a specific area, (2) enhanced with years in the organization and in the industry, (3) improved with successes that have been publicly recognized

- *Reputation:* (1) affected by personality thought to be "difficult," "easy-going," "fair," "honest," or other traits; (2) influenced by an image that is attractive or unattractive; (3) affected by a track record of success or failure

- *Goodwill:* (1) created by favorable or unfavorable opinion built over time with specific individuals or groups, (2) generated (often) by providing benefits to audience

4. Has different objectives

A fourth characteristic of managerial persuasion is that—in contrast to the kind of persuasion that deals with selling products—managerial persuasion deals with changing workplace behavior, gaining compliance, and creating agreement.

Changing behavior: Consider these two important issues when dealing with a problem concerning someone's behavior: encouragement for change and documentation of the problem.

- *Encouragement for change:* Communication involving behavior is strongly persuasive, and to the extent that you can encourage change, the problem will improve. Creating motivation for change involves choosing your language wisely and reaching a balance between encouragement and threat of consequences. In case the problem does not improve, though, it is necessary to provide documentation of the problem and what you are doing about it.

- *Documentation of the problem:* Documentation will include stating observed problems and illustrating them with evidence. Here are some examples of managerial responsibilities dealing with employee behavior: (1) dealing with an employee who doesn't do her/his job adequately; (2) dealing with an employee who doesn't work well with others; (3) handling performance appraisals; (4) helping an employee understand the limits of his/her authority.

Documentation is necessary in cases where oral and written encouragement for change have not been effective, and you need to provide written evidence of the problem and how you have handled it. Stating problems and supporting them with appropriate evidence will be covered in the following chapters.

Gaining compliance: Although you will often think that the policy changes and other administrative news that you give employees are simply informational, you will always be persuading at some level. Employees not only need to understand a new policy but also must be willing to comply with it. Important issues to consider are *power bases*—how much power the manager or message sender has; *verbal strategies*—language choices made by the message sender; and *overall tactics*—those strategies used to overcome resistance. If you have employees working for you, some of the communication responsibilities you will have include the following: (1) explaining and creating "buy-in" for changes in operations or changes in policy; (2) explaining negative news in regard to subordinate group requests; (3) creating ways to increase employee productivity.

Dealing with groups of employees and dealing with individuals require similar skills, but in addition, they also require a deep understanding of how to achieve "buy-in." Ultimately, without employees' agreement with objectives developed by managers, the organization's goals will probably not be met.

Creating agreement: When working with peers, superiors, or groups from other organizations, you must be able to promote agreement by using appropriate appeals. With a superior, a colleague, or someone in another organization, you should carefully select claims and evidence to provide the kinds of appeals you believe will be appropriate. Making these choices requires preparation, knowledge, and a strong ability to communicate.

Some common tasks in this area are: (1) justifying an increase in funding for a project; (2) presenting results of a project to superiors, including board members; (3) presenting negative information; (4) asking for more staff, more resources, or more time; (5) convincing team members to adopt a particular procedure; (6) persuading a client company to choose your strategy for chance of growth.

When you think about the kinds of appeals you need, consider the reasons, evidence, and connections you will use to persuade and/or influence outcomes. The concepts of reasons, evidence, and connections are discussed in depth in the next two chapters.

The figure below illustrates a useful way to visualize managerial persuasion. Think of yourself in the middle of a large sphere. Your abilities to create a logical message, to motivate your audience, and to enhance your credibility all interact to comprise the core of your persuasiveness. However, this core lies within and is affected by the organizational environment (shown by the larger circle) and the country culture (shown by the even larger circle).

In this book, we will discuss each of the components of this illustration in turn: the logical message in Chapters I and II, the motivated audience in Chapters III and IV, your enhanced credibility in Chapter IV, the organizational environment in Chapter V, and the country culture in Chapter VI.

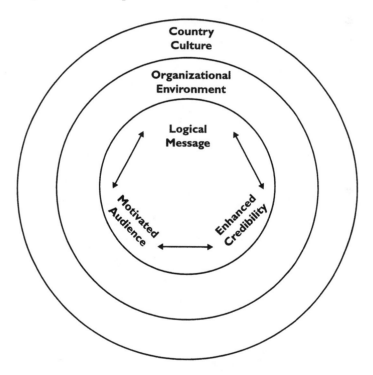

CHAPTER I OUTLINE

   I. State your position

  II. State your reasons

 III. State your evidence for each reason
  1. Differentiating reasons and evidence
  2. Choosing kinds of evidence
  3. Evaluating the effectiveness of evidence

 IV. Make clear connections
  1. Defining connections
  2. Recognizing implicit versus explicit connections

CHAPTER I

Develop Your Argument

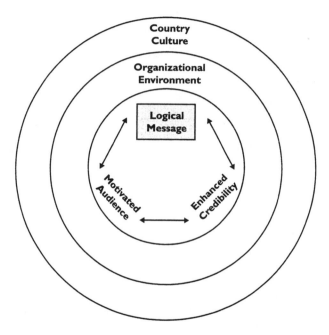

O ne of the important aspects of managerial persuasion has to do with creating a logical message, as highlighted in the gray box above. Creating such a message involves the art of "argumentation." Used in this sense, argumentation does not mean having an argument or disagreement with someone—but rather being able to (1) take a position, (2) support it with reasoning, (3) support your reasoning with evidence, and (4) make clear connections among your ideas. This chapter covers techniques for enhancing your effectiveness in each of these four areas.

I. STATE YOUR POSITION

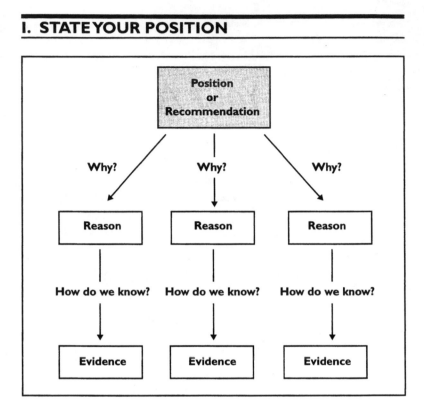

Although it may seem obvious that you need to state your position (or recommendation), many people who are trying to persuade either forget to do so or do not state it clearly enough. Consider the following quotation from a manager who had decided to offer his department flextime: " I've given a lot of consideration to flextime, and I'd like to give you my thoughts on the issue."

Based on this statement, his employees, some of whom did not favor flextime, thought that the issue was still open and that they might be able to influence the final decision. They wasted a lot of time in a meeting on the issue before the employees figured out that the manager had already made the decision. He could have made things simpler by stating his position clearly.

How do you state a position or recommendation clearly? In general, you need to include words that show what you want to happen in terms of numbers, timing, and/or actions. Consider the following examples:

Unclear	This department may need more money next year.
Clear	This department needs an additional $50,000 in its budget for next year.
Unclear	To address the problem on line 4 of the new injection molding plant, we should think about works in progress.
Clear	To eliminate the bottleneck on line 4 of the new injection molding plant, reduce the number of works in progress from 25 to 15.
Unclear	This department is considering the flextime issue.
Clear	Beginning Monday, July 11, this department will offer flextime schedules for all employees.

Once you have a clear position statement, you need to support it with reasons and evidence.

II. STATE YOUR REASONS

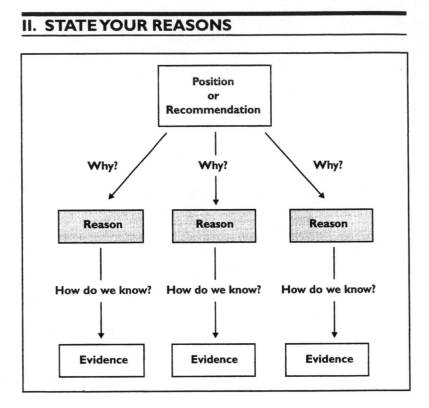

 A reason is the "why" part of your message that follows your position statement. It may seem obvious that you need to provide reasons for your positions, but because reasons can be more difficult than you would think, many people omit them without realizing it.

 Consider the following statement from a manager of information systems: "Although we all know that moving from our current IS platform to the new XY platform will cause some problems, I'm going to recommend it at Friday's meeting, and I'd like your support." This manager has forgotten to state her reason, which may be simply that in spite of the possible problems, changing to a new platform will benefit the company in certain ways. She could then say what those ways are and provide evidence to show that what she says is correct.

Always state your reasons in terms of audience benefits, that is, "what's in it for them." In addition, each reason must have a logical relationship to the overall position. The following examples show reasons that are benefits to the audience and have a logical relationship to the position taken to support a small company's decision to change its medical coverage for employees:

- The new system will provide an opportunity to personalize your benefits, and in some cases, get more coverage. *(This reason provides a direct benefit to each employee and is directly related to the stated change.)*

- Unlike our current system, co-pays will not be required except for those with the greatest needs. *(This reason provides a benefit to most employees—no more co-pays—and the same but nothing worse for others. It also is directly related to the policy change.)*

- The new system will help the company improve its bottom line and in doing that, will ensure continued benefits now and in the future. *(This reason is directly related to the change, and it also benefits each employee by promising stability for future benefits.)*

Sometimes, what is stated as a reason is not directly related to the issue under discussion, or is a part of the evidence rather than an actual reason. Consider the following examples:

- The company has looked at all operating expenses and is also making changes in its salary structure. *(The issue of operating expenses as a whole and making changes in other areas is not directly related to the change in medical compensation. This would not answer the "why" part of the question on the issue of this change.)*

- In the brochure you will each receive, you will see a number of options along with an explanation of each. *(This is not a reason for making the change nor does it explicitly indicate a benefit. It simply describes one aspect of the change.)*

Clearly stated reasons that are directly related to the position and that indicate benefits to the audience are a crucial component in persuasion.

III. STATE YOUR EVIDENCE
FOR EACH REASON

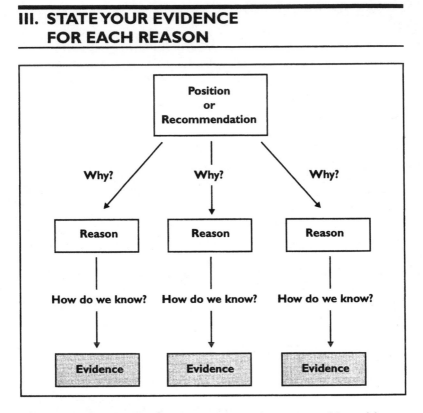

In a persuasive message, each reason must be supported by evidence. Sometimes the difference between reasons and evidence is hard to identify.

Consider the following quote from a department manager: "We've decided to install a time clock and require each of you to punch in because last week I noticed that over a third of you were late— some of you up to an hour." This information is a piece of evidence that could support a reason such as ". . . because many of you are routinely coming to work late." This could then be followed by "For example, just last week . . . etc."

A reason is more general than the evidence that supports it, and the process moves from the abstract to the concrete. Think of a reason as the answer to "why?" Facts, figures, and details of an explanation generally comprise evidence that supports a reason. Think of evidence as the answer to the "how do you know?" question.

I. Differentiating reasons and evidence

The following chart illustrates the differences between reasons and evidence on the issue of keeping a department lunchroom rather than turning it into an information systems office.

Reasons	Evidence
Reasons = Why I take this position....	**Evidence = I know this because....**
We need a lunchroom on the premises.	• Almost everyone uses it for either lunch or for cool drinks, coffee and tea, and snacks. • Most of the secretaries eat lunch in the lunchroom because they can't afford to eat out every day. • The lunchroom provides the secretaries a place to keep their lunches cool, heat them up, and eat away from their desks. This allows them to feel more refreshed when they go back to work.
Morale is suffering because of the possibility of losing the lunchroom.	• My secretary told me that everyone is upset and that they feel their needs are being ignored. • This situation follows a series of unpopular demands on them, such as no raises last year and being asked to park at the farthest end of the lot. • One secretary has resigned and others are considering it.
The costs are a problem.	• It will cost $100,000 to remove the lunchroom and put in the new system and office equipment. • Replacing a secretary costs up to twice their average salary if you consider interviewing, hiring, and training; this would be a minimum of $25,000 per secretary. • There are cost issues connected with a drop in productivity; having to train a new secretary causes a temporary drop in productivity. Low morale also causes a productivity drop.

2. Choosing kinds of evidence

You can choose from among the following kinds of evidence, based on what you believe will appeal to the receivers of your message. You have the following kinds of support to consider:

Evidence that proves includes three categories:

- *Numbers:* Numerical evidence includes cost information as well as statistics. Cost information might be any numbers that refer to financial value, profits, and losses; statistics must be valid and relevant.
- *Facts:* Simple facts that are easily confirmed can provide strong support as evidence. When facts are generally known by the audience or are easily verified, they may not need further support; however, some "facts" are actually claims that need verification. Facts generated by research can also prove whether or not the research is explained adequately.
- *Expert testimony:* This includes evidence you get from others, either from published data or from interviews with people recognized as knowledgeable on your issue, or your own observation or experience.

Evidence that explains includes several other categories of information:

- *Examples:* Examples and incidences that have occurred to you or others and are relevant to your issue can be used to help support your decision. Hypothetical examples can also be used to illustrate your points.
- *Benchmarking:* Information on what other organizations are doing on the issue you are dealing with can help you to be persuasive.
- *Research:* This support deals with the research that you have done or is reported on the issue of your position or recommendation. Research can lead to facts that can prove, but the research itself may need explanation.
- *Comparisons and contrasts:* A comparison can help you explain similarities; contrasts will help you explain differences.
- *Clarifying information:* This category includes summaries, restatements, and definitions.

Of course, some evidence can serve as proof and can help explain, depending on the circumstances and the evidence itself. Some kinds of evidence that can serve both needs include expert testimony, real examples, and personal experience.

3. Evaluating the effectiveness of evidence

Make sure that each piece of evidence you use is valid and your sources are objective and competent. If your evidence is not effective, you may lose credibility and put your whole argument at risk.

Validity of evidence: (1) Is the evidence consistent with other known evidence? (2) Can it be verified? (3) Is the information current?

Objectivity and competence of the source: (1) Does the source have an interest in the event or evidence cited? (2) Is the source known to be biased on the issue? (3) Does the source have good credentials for the issue at hand? (4) Was the source in a position to know or observe what he/she is saying?

The chart below summarizes your choices of evidence and how to make it valid and objective.

VALIDITY AND OBJECTIVITY OF EVIDENCE	
Evidence that proves	
Numbers	Costs must be verifiable; statistics must be valid and relevant.
Facts	Some facts must be verified.
Expert testimony	Source must be objective (have no vested interest or bias) and competent (credentials relevant to issue, in a position to know the truth of the situation).
Evidence that explains	
Examples	Must be relevant and analogous to situation.
Benchmarking	Must be comparable to your situation, current, and relevant.
Research	Must be verifiable, current, and applicable.
Comparisons and contrasts	Items compared and contrasted must be analogous.
Clarifying information	Must include familiar language and facts that are easily understood.

IV. MAKE CLEAR CONNECTIONS

To persuade others effectively, it isn't enough to be clear about your
position, state strong reasons, and provide good evidence. You must
also be sure that you have made the necessary connections between
your position/recommendation and your reasons and evidence. This
section deals with recognizing what connections are and when you
need to state them explicitly.

In the chart below, the bold two-sided arrows illustrate the different kinds of connections you need to make.

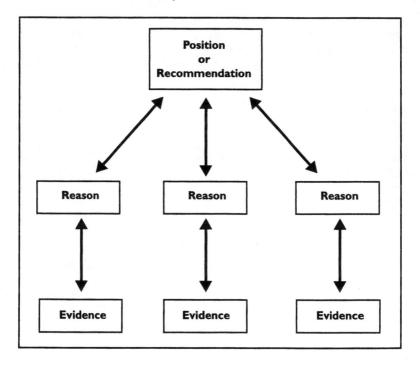

1. Defining connections

To ensure that your audience understands your position in the way you wish, you need to provide connections between the components of your message. You need to provide these connections as shown in the illustration on the facing page and explained below.

To tie your evidence to your reason. Connections that tie your evidence to your reason show how the evidence supports the reason you are providing. They fill in the ideas of "because of" or "since" or "given that." These connections do not add new information, but rather show the relationship between the reason and the evidence.

To tie your reasons and evidence to your position. Connections in this situation answer the question, "How does the reason support the position?" Like the connections above, they do not add new information, but rather show relationships.

2. Recognizing implicit versus explicit connections

Some connections need to be stated and some do not. When the relationship between the position and reasons/evidence or between the reason and evidence is not completely clear, you will need to state your connections.

Implicit connections: Many times, your connections are so clear that they don't need to be stated. Consider the following examples:

> *Example:* Going to flextime will please our employees (**reason**). Most of the people in my department want to go to flextime (**general evidence**). A survey we gave two weeks ago shows that 22 out of 25 employees were in favor of instituting flextime as soon as possible (**specific evidence**).

The connection between the above reason and evidence is implied because the relationship between the two is obvious.

> *Example:* I recommend we go to flextime as soon as possible (**position**). Going to flextime will improve morale (**reason**).

In the second example, the connection between position and reason is implied; the relationship between the position and the reason is obvious because no one would argue that improved morale is not a good thing and that working conditions do not affect morale.

Explicit connections: Other times, however, you need to state your connections explicitly because the relationships between either the position and reason or between the reasons and evidence are not as clear.

> *Example:* I recommend abandoning the plan to remove the secretaries' lunchroom to make space for an IS center (**position**). One reason for my view is that the secretaries are angry about this plan (**reason**). Angry secretaries can cause us a lot of problems, including a drop in morale and productivity (**connection**).

Some audiences would see the connection between angry secretaries and morale, but others would need the connection to be pointed out. It is not obvious that angry secretaries would affect a department's productivity; they might be used to grumbling about things, and your audience may be used to overlooking secretaries' feelings about the work environment.

> *Example:* Going to flextime will increase the department's productivity (**reason**). Most of the employees in the department want to go to

flextime. The results of a recent survey show that 22 out of 25 people are in favor of instituting flextime as soon as possible (**evidence**). If we can satisfy our employees on this issue, morale should improve, and improved morale can lead to increased productivity (**connection**).

In this example, you need to state the connection because there is a gap between the productivity issue stated in the reason and the desires of the employees stated in the evidence. The morale issue can provide the bridge between the two.

Mixture: implicit and explicit connections in one argument: Sometimes, a position will include a number of points, some of which have implied connections while others need to be stated. The example below argues that XYZ company should market its administrative health care services in Argentina. Parts of the argument require the connection to be stated explicitly:

Point #1:

Reason: Argentina's health care market needs these services.

Evidence: Seventy percent of the country's hospitals have reported management problems.

Connection: (Implied between reason and evidence.)

Point #2:

Reason: Argentina wants these services.

Evidence: Last year 40 percent of the hospitals and health care facilities contracted out their administrative management.

Connection: (Implied between reason and evidence.)

Point #3:

Reason: XYZ's services fit the needs of this market.

Evidence: (Insert explanation of XYZ's competencies.)

Connection between reasons and evidence: (Explicit) XYZ's core competencies and experience in North American markets can help solve the problems the health care market is experiencing.

Connection between position and reasons: (Explicit) By supplying the needs for this new region, XYZ will experience positive growth, increase profits, and avoid a possible loss due to a downturn in the U.S. health care market.

To summarize, if you want to justify a position (or recommendation), you need to be able to articulate reasons, provide evidence that the reasons are valid, and show how the evidence is connected to the reason and/or the reason is connected to the position. The following dialogue illustrates these principles:

> YOU: My position is that we should institute flextime (**position**).

> AUDIENCE: *Why* do you think flextime is a good thing for this organization?

> YOU: *Because* the majority of the employees are in favor of flextime (**reason**).

> AUDIENCE: *How do you know* the majority of the employees want flextime?

> YOU: I know this is true because we did a survey with a 90 percent response rate that showed that 93 percent of the respondents were in favor of moving to flextime (**evidence**).

> AUDIENCE: *So why does this matter?*

> YOU: This is important because accommodating our employees' wishes on this issue will have a positive effect on morale, and thus potentially, on productivity (**connection**).

CHECKLIST: DEVELOPING YOUR ARGUMENT

Evaluating position statement

✓ Do you state your position or recommendation explicitly?

✓ Is your statement clear with specific actions included?

Evaluating reasons

✓ Do your reasons answer the question "Why" in reference to your position?

✓ Are they stated explicitly?

✓ Are they relevant and useful, addressing key issues?

✓ Are they clearly connected to your position?

Evaluating evidence

✓ Do you have evidence for each reason?

✓ Does your evidence answer the question "How do you know?"

✓ Do you have enough detail in your evidence to support your reason?

✓ Is your evidence well developed, using both general and specific data when appropriate?

✓ Is your evidence relevant to the reason it is supporting?

Evaluating connections

✓ Do you need to be explicit in the connections between your position and your reasons?

✓ Do your reasons and evidence have an obvious relationship or do you need to state it explicitly?

✓ Is the "So what?" factor obvious in your message or do you need to spell it out?

CHAPTER II OUTLINE

I. Focus on your message structure
   1. Choosing a pattern
   2. Maintaining internal logic

II. Avoid unfair and illogical arguments
   1. Avoiding unfair evidence
   2. Avoiding illogical reasoning
   3. Avoiding misleading charts and graphs

CHAPTER II

Check Your Logic

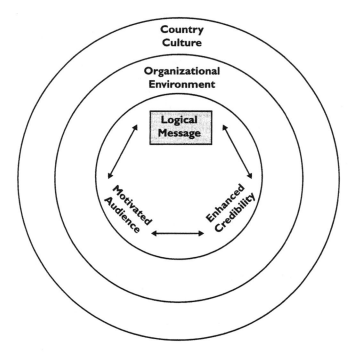

Once you have clarified your position, reasons, and evidence, you are halfway toward creating a persuasive message. To enhance your message even further, you will need to (1) focus on your message structure, and (2) avoid unfair and illogical arguments—both of which are covered in this chapter.

I. FOCUS ON YOUR MESSAGE STRUCTURE

How your message hangs together—that is, how coherently you get your points across—is to a great degree determined by your overall organizational pattern.

1. Choosing a pattern

The pattern you choose should be based on your audience and the circumstances of your message, but generally you have three choices: direct, indirect, or modified direct. If your message is short, you may choose any of the three options. If not, think about when to use each of them as explained below.

Direct: In a direct pattern, you state your position or recommendation first. You follow your statement of position or recommendation with your reasons and evidence. If you state your decision anywhere in the first two sentences, you are using a direct organizational pattern.

> *Example of direct pattern*
>> This department will institute flextime beginning July 1.
>> [followed by reasons and evidence]

Choose the direct pattern most of the time in a business setting—except when you know that your audience will disagree with your position or recommendation.

Indirect: In the indirect pattern, you state your reasons and evidence first and end with your position or recommendation statement. In this pattern, you either state your decision at the very end of the message or somewhere in the final section.

> *Example of indirect pattern*
>> We have recently studied the issue of how to increase efficiency... [followed by evidence and reasons] Therefore, we have decided to institute flextime beginning July 1.

Choose the indirect pattern when your audience disagrees with your decision or recommendation.

Modified direct: When you use this organizational pattern, start with information that is neutral, attention-getting, or context-setting. Then, follow with your position/recommendation statement, then your reasons and evidence. Your position/recommendation statement can come as early as the third or fourth sentence or as late as the second paragraph in a written message; generally, it comes within the first third of the message.

> *Example of modified direct pattern*
> The HR department has reviewed our need to increase efficiency. Among the many alternatives we considered, flextime looks promising for many reasons. Therefore, we are going to institute flextime beginning...

You might choose the modified direct pattern if your audience knows the situation well or if they disagree with your position/recommendation.

2. Maintaining internal logic

Your overall pattern is not the only important aspect of a persuasive message. To make such a message clear and compelling, you also need a logical internal structure. This means providing reasons that follow logically from one to the other. Many people simply provide a so-called "laundry list" of reasons, or points in random order, to support a position. An ideal structure, however, will show a tightly organized and coherent set of reasons and evidence.

Consider the following list of reasons to institute flextime in an automotive plant:

Ineffective: laundry list order

- We could save money.
- Productivity could rise.
- Morale will improve.
- Employees have asked for more control over their schedules.

Although the reasons above have some relation to one another, the order in which they are listed obscures their connections. These connections are more transparent below:

Effective: logical order showing connections between ideas

- Employees have asked for more control over their schedules.
  (Giving employees what they have asked for will affect morale, which leads to the next reason.)
- Morale will improve.
  (Morale will improve because you are giving employees what they have asked for; and if morale improves, the next reason is relevant.)
- Productivity could rise.
  (If productivity rises as a result of improved morale, then the next point is logical.)
- We could save money.

II. AVOID UNFAIR AND ILLOGICAL ARGUMENTS

In addition to providing a clear overall structure, you also need to avoid unfair and illogical reasoning if you want to be persuasive. As a businessperson, your persuasiveness is closely connected to your long-term and ongoing relationship with your audience. A message that is unfair, illogical, or misleading will affect your credibility and your long-term ability to get things done.

1. Avoiding unfair evidence

Unfairness in evidence can fall into four categories:

Quoting out of context: This refers to the practice of taking a segment of a written or oral message that appears to support a certain conclusion but which if presented in its entirety would not support that conclusion.

> *Example:* The secretaries have said that they are unhappy and that we are not sensitive to their needs. They seem to be deliberately ignoring all the positive things about working for this department.

Distortion: This is often called a "straw man" argument because the information at issue is made into a straw man (something easily destroyed) or distorted in such a way that it is easily refuted.

> *Example:* If we give in to the secretaries' latest demand to maintain the current lunchroom, we'll be setting ourselves up to be completely controlled by their constant demands. They've complained about their salaries and their parking facilities and now about the lunchroom. What's next in their list of constant demands?

Slanting: This entails suppressing facts unfavorable to your position; if your audience discovers the missing facts later, your credibility will be decreased.

> *Example:* Our secretaries have been treated very well by this department, and this demand to keep the current lunchroom in spite of the department's needs to put in a new IS system in that space seems to have come out of nowhere.

Name-calling: This is a personal attack on another person or an appeal to an audience's prejudices rather than to reason. This technique is often called an "ad hominem" argument.

> *Example:* I hate to say this, but our secretaries have become spoiled whiners who are trying to usurp our authority to run the department in the most efficient way. They don't need a lunchroom any more than the rest of us do, and they have the same lunch break everyone has, so why are they constantly complaining?

2. Avoiding illogical reasoning

Unfairness in arguments has to do with misleading or dishonest information. Illogical arguments have to do with reasoning and can be labeled in various ways. Regardless of the label, though, the information that follows defines and illustrates some of the main problems in reasoning. You can see these reasoning problems in many current newspaper and magazine articles as well as in many books that seek to persuade. The nine categories below define the problems and show examples:

Ignoring the burden of proof: to state a claim and provide no evidence whatsoever to support it.

> *Example:* All of us know that changing our medical benefits provider will entail some problems, but I think it's the best thing for us to do. The other alternatives are not as attractive. I have given the matter a lot of thought and this choice seems to me to be the best we can do. I am going to recommend this change at our next managers' meeting, and I would like you to support me.

Begging the question: to (1) make a claim based on an assumption which itself must be proved; or (2) use circular reasoning where the claim is restated as the conclusion.

> *Examples:* Smith shouldn't get a raise this year. He didn't get one last year, and if he didn't deserve it then, he doesn't deserve it now (**assuming what has to be proved**). The division's refusal to accept a proposal on flextime will cause low morale because employees will be unhappy with working conditions (**circular reasoning**).

Hasty generalization: to draw a conclusion from too small a sample or from a sample not likely to be typical.

> *Example:* Employees here are not putting in their required 40 hours per week. Last week, two people were late punching their time clocks.

Red herring: to shift or broaden the evidence at hand to include examples not pertinent to the issue. (from an eighteenth-century term used in fox hunting, the red herring distracts the audience from the main issue.)

> *Example:* Most of the people who are upset about our new policy regarding smoking in the offices are smokers who feel they are being punished because of their habit. I agree with them and think we'd be better off concentrating our effort on the pollution produced by automobiles, since they cause more air pollution than smoking does.

False division and either/or logic: to limit choices by including everything in a small number of groups (e.g., there are three kinds of people), or to only two (e.g, either you do this or that), ignoring other alternatives.

> *Examples:* There are three kinds of people in this office: those who work hard and get their jobs done, those who seem to work hard but don't get their jobs done, and those who don't work hard and don't get their jobs done (**limiting choices**).

> Either we go to flextime or we resign ourselves to losing staff and productivity (**either/or**).

Appeal to popular opinion: to offer as evidence statements such as "everybody knows" or "all intelligent people believe that . . . "

> *Example:* Everybody knows that this company was on its way to bankruptcy until Smith took over, and the employees who know how to achieve objectives will support my proposal.

Causal generalization: to attribute a cause to an event or problem that is not completely satisfied by the facts; also referred to as "sequential fallacy."

> *Example:* The reconfiguration team was initially successful. The problems started when the accounting people became involved. It may have been a mistake to bring in the accounting people at this point.

False analogy: to compare two things that are not similar in essential ways to the conclusion being drawn.

> *Example:* If people in this organization can be anywhere in the world and still communicate with each other, why can't the union negotiators and company representatives communicate with each other and come up with a reasonable contract?

Oversimplification: to apply a simple answer to a complex problem or to recognize only one of several causes of an effect.

> *Example:* The reason the company has been losing money for the last four quarters is the lack of customer service in the individual stores.

3. Avoiding misleading charts and graphs

In addition to avoiding problems with unfair and illogical evidence, you should also avoid misleading charts, graphs, and other visual aids. The consequences of distortions in visuals include loss of credibility and a decrease in your ability to persuade and influence change over time. Among the innumerable ways to mislead with visual aids and with statistics are not using zero for the baseline, distorting the grid, omitting a scale, and using three-dimensional effects. The illustrations below are based on communication expert Scot Ober and others. (See the bibliography for further details.)

Not using zero for the baseline: The bar chart on the left below starts with zero on the value axis; the distorted chart on the right starts with 50. The distorted chart is misleading; for example, the third column looks much shorter than the second.

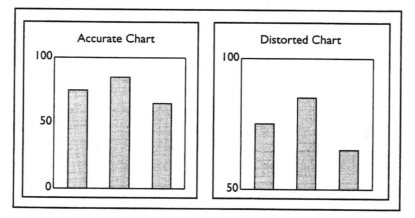

Distorting the grid: The accurate chart below has a grid of squares. The two distorted line charts show how data can be made to look more or less serious by stretching the grid horizontally or by stretching it vertically.

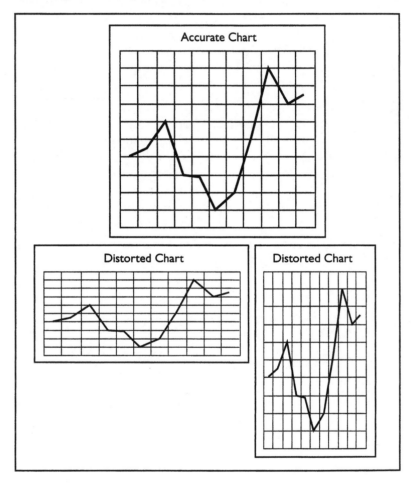

Using an axis unrepresentative of the data: The distortion on the y axis of the second of these charts makes the grid unrepresentative of the time periods of the data.

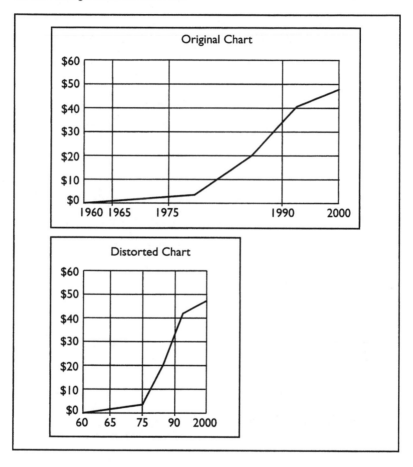

Not providing a scale: Since there's no scale on the distorted chart below, there is no way to know the precise relationship between the three sets of data

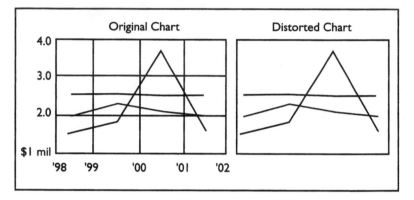

Using 3D effects: Another problem is caused by the lack of clarity in three-dimensional objects. Three-dimensional graphs do not clearly display the data because the third dimension distorts the size of some of the wedges. For example, the 3D bar charts below hide the true relationship among the bars because parts of them are hidden.

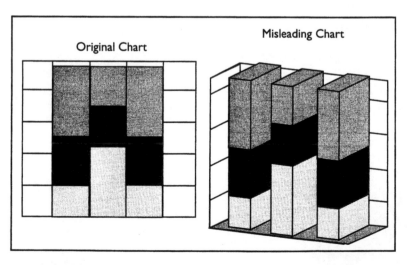

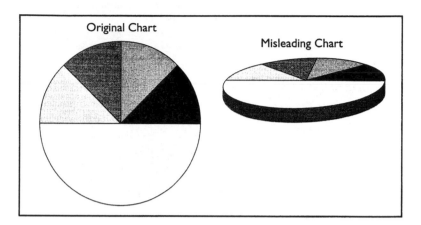

Paying attention to the details of your argument and making sure you have avoided illogical reasoning and misleading visual aids will help you maintain your credibility and enhance your persuasiveness.

CHECKLIST: CHECKING YOUR LOGIC

Focus on your message structure

✓ Identify and choose a pattern: direct, indirect, or modified direct.

✓ Maintain internal logic.

Motivate your audience

✓ Avoid unfair evidence (quoting out of context, distortion, slanting, and name-calling).

✓ Avoid illogical reasoning (ignoring the burden of proof, begging the question, hasty generalization, red herring, false division, appeal to popular opinion, causal generalization, false analogy, and oversimplification).

✓ Avoid misleading charts and graphs (non-zero baseline, distorted grid, unrepresentative axis, no scale, and 3D effects).

CHAPTER III OUTLINE

I. Questions to ask
   1. Who are they?
   2. What is their personality type?

II. Approaches to consider
   1. Cultivate listening skills
   2. Put your listening skills to work
   3. Learn to read carefully
   4. Put your reading skills to work

CHAPTER III

Analyze Your Audience

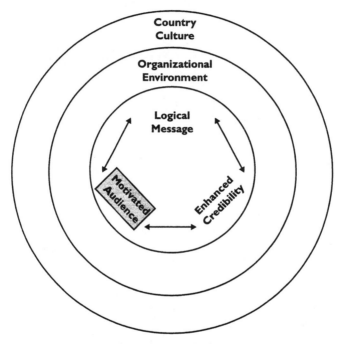

Having a logical message, as we've discussed in the first two chapters, is not enough for successful persuasion. A second aspect of persuasion has to do with appealing to your particular audience—as highlighted in gray on the figure above. The word "audience" refers to the person or people you are trying to persuade, in both written and oral communication.

To analyze your audience effectively, consider the following: (1) questions to ask and (2) approaches to use to answer those questions.

I. QUESTIONS TO ASK

The better you know your audience, the more effective you will be in
persuading them of your point of view and influencing their actions.
To begin your analysis, you should ask yourself the following questions.

1. Who are they?

Your audience may be one person or many people, all of whom have
personal characteristics, opinions about you and your topic of concern, and expectations about how they like to receive information.
Study your audience with the following in mind:

Who are my primary, secondary, and other audiences?

- *Primary audience* will be the person(s) who directly receives your
  message. Most often the decision maker, the person with control over
  the outcome of your message, will be included in your primary audience.

- *Secondary audience* will be those who will hear, read, or come to
  know through informal communication what you have communicated. This audience may be affected by your message in some way
  and may have the power to help or hinder your objectives.

- *Other audiences may* include a "gatekeeper," the person through
  whom you must send your message, as well as anyone who may have
  influence with your broader audience's opinions.

What do they know about the subject of your message?
Consider which of the following "Five W's Plus How" your audience
needs to know to fully understand the issue and your reasoning.
(1) *Who* is involved in and affected by this decision? (2) *What* is the
decision and its implications? (3) *Where* in the organization will the
decision have the most impact? (4) *When* will any potential changes
take place? (4) *Why* is it necessary? (5) *How* will it be implemented?

- *If your audience is knowledgeable:* If your audience already knows
  the background of your message, you don't need to tell them about it.
  Giving your audience a lot of background information they already
  know may cause them to lose interest before you fully explain your
  position, and thus reduce your persuasive appeal.

- *If your audience lacks knowledge:* On the other hand, if your audience knows nothing, then you will need more information to provide the basis for your points. If you do not provide enough background for your audience to understand your decision and reasons for it, you will not persuade them. In this case, you will have to explain further, answer questions, and in some cases, restate your decision with reasons and supporting evidence.

- *If you have a mixed audience:* Sometimes your audience consists of more than one person with varying degrees of knowledge, or you don't know how much your audience understands about the issue. In these cases, take a middle road and provide enough context to make sense of your argument, but do not include so much information that you lose your audience before you get to your points. In this case, you might provide an attachment of background information if your message is written or a handout if your message is delivered orally.

What is their opinion?   Your audience may have a range of opinions on the issue and your decision regarding it. These opinions can include caring or not caring about the issue or agreeing, being neutral, or disagreeing, as in the matrix below:

REACTION MATRIX			
	Agreeing		
	Agree	Neutral	Disagree
Caring Care a lot about issue		Example 1	
Care somewhat			
Ambivalent—agree at times, disagree at times			
Don't care about issue			Example 2

Although it may seem contradictory, a person can care about an issue but be neutral about the decision regarding it.

Example #1: If you're being assigned one of two new offices, and both are large and have windows, you probably won't care too much which office you get. Similarly, someone who does not care about an issue can agree or disagree with the decision made regarding it.

Example #2: The manager in the department where the lunchroom for secretaries is in question would not be personally affected by the decision but might still have an opinion. In this case, the person is not invested in the issue but believes the decision is good or bad in an abstract way

- *If your audience agrees with you* on the topic, your job as a persuader is easier, and you will probably not have to provide as much information and support for your points.

- *If your audience disagrees with you,* the burden of persuasion is on you to provide reasons, explanation, and support that make convincing appeals.

- *If your audience has no opinion* on, but high interest in, your topic, you also have to provide adequate information to be persuasive. However, if your audience has no opinion and little interest in the topic, you will need to show why the topic is important to them and provide more attention-getting strategies.

What are their preferred channels?   The term "channels" of communication refers to your communication medium—such as writing, email, phone calls, meetings, presentations, and so on. Consider your audience's expectations and their preferred channels of communication to help you decide on a persuasive strategy. For example,

- Does your audience prefer face-to-face meetings over emails or paper memos?
- Does your audience like small talk and socializing?
- Do meetings led by your audience tend to run long with important issues not addressed until the end?
- Does your audience prefer formal or informal communication?
- Does your audience dislike messages longer than one page?

Another strategy is to use a channel that is unusual and unexpected for your audience. Remember, however, that doing the unexpected can be persuasive and compelling, if done carefully. To be able to use surprise and the unexpected to help you persuade, it's even more important to know what the "expected" would be for each audience. The two questions to answer in this case are (1) What does my audience expect in this situation? and (2) How much difference from the expected can my audience tolerate?

What are their constraints?   Realistically, your audience will have constraints that affect their response to your decision and how you deliver it. Some of these constraints might include:

- *Timing:* They may have little time to spend reading/listening and understanding your reasoning.
- *Distractions:* They may be distracted by the other demands in their work.
- *Low priority:* They may give your message low priority because of a number of factors, including your relationship to them, your status in the organization, and their own time constraints

If you believe that your message may not get attention due to any of the above reasons, you should use a strategy to arouse interest, choose a channel that provides immediate interaction (such as face-to-face), or plan to deliver your message at a more appropriate time.

2. What is their personality type?

People cope with the world in individual ways, developed over time and based on experience and education. For example, some like details, and some are impatient with them. Some need lots of facts and figures in order to make a decision. Some think positively about most people, and some are typically skeptical about others and their motives. Researchers Hart, Quinn, Rogers, and Hildebrandt (all cited in the bibliography) have developed a useful typology for assessing personality roles in the workplace. (Naturally, everyone has a combination of these roles and may exhibit different roles at different times.) The four roles are:

Creator: The creator personality is able to see the big picture and consider strategic choices in any given situation. People with this kind of personality focus on ideas rather than details and provide a sense of identity and common aims for participants. Use the following techniques to persuade this kind of person:

- *Oral:* enthusiasm, movement, unconventional words, overt encouragement
- *Written:* abstract words and ideas, unconventional formats and message channels, positive language

Fact-finder: Fact-finder personalities want to be involved in all the minutiae of a situation. They often expect regular progress reports with specific details for every aspect of a problem or procedure. At times, this kind of personality can be overbearing and lead to "micromanaging" or "looking over an employee's shoulder." On the other hand, sometimes they can help people think through issues, handle problems, or provide direction. Use the following techniques to persuade this kind of person:

- *Oral:* controlled voice and movement, lots of information and specific details in support of a position
- *Written:* lots of information including context of the situation and reasons and support for a position, routine types of message channels, conventional formats

Analyst: The analyst takes a step back and reviews how a project is progressing and how the work process is developing. This type of person observes carefully and intercedes when the process hits a snag. Details and support for a position are important to an analyst, but the main focus is on whether or not each decision in the project makes sense and if the outcome is likely to fit the objectives of the situation. Use the following techniques to persuade this kind of person:

- *Oral:* well-organized, generally objective or neutral in tone, logical, calm vocal expression, and little movement
- *Written:* conventional formats, well-organized, clear language with a focus on logic and reasoning

Judge: The judge role expresses the conviction that there is an ideal way to proceed and seeks to motivate others to fulfill this view. A judge is adept at creating rapport with those involved in a project and generating enthusiasm for the process. A businessperson who must play this role does so when a project falters because of external, unforeseeable factors and when the process disintegrates because of employee problems. Use the following techniques to persuade this kind of person:

- *Oral:* enthusiastic and warm, open movements, use of examples, and emotional appeals
- *Written:* friendly tone, informal language and formats, personal message channels, use of examples, and emotional appeals

The table on the following page summarizes these personality types.

PERSONALITY TYPES

Motivating philosophy	Communication habits	Persuade by
CREATOR		
• Life is exciting and wonderful. • Change is good and new ideas are desirable.	• Can generate ideas for every situation • Dominates conversation • Focuses on broad situation as opposed to details • Astute in recognizing main issue • Makes errors in facts but often unaware of it • Likes pictures, charts, and other graphic aids	• Focusing on big picture and opportunities • Using words that suggest creativity and imagination • Listening carefully • Showing enthusiasm
FACT-FINDER		
• Decisions should be based on facts. • Properly supported facts are absolute and not to be questioned.	• Fills messages with details • Logical and generally unemotional • Can communicate in a neutral way and often clearly • Precise in word choices • Wants factual support for all premises	• Documenting assertions and sources of information • Using inductive approach (go from facts to conclusions) • Showing objectivity with neutral words • Using control in speaking and writing
ANALYST		
• Life is rational. • Most problems can be solved by logic and reasoning.	• Presents arguments supported by data • Organizes messages carefully • Separates positives and negatives • Analyzes situation before reaching conclusion and may be slow in making decision • Uses linear reasoning	• Using logic and linear sentence constructions • Showing cause and effect • Focusing on relationships between components • Breaking issue apart into constituent components
JUDGE		
• Each situation needs to be evaluated before acting. • Fairness can be a problem and needs to be carefully considered.	• Weighs words carefully • Either agrees or disagrees • Is aware of status and power • Thinks about incentives, advantages, disadvantages • Considers "value" of proposition	• Focusing on establishing relationship • Showing pros and cons • Using ethical and emotional appeals • Being willing to compromise

II. APPROACHES TO CONSIDER

How can you answer the audience analysis questions posed in the previous section? You can (1) cultivate your listening skills and (2) learn to read carefully. If you are a good listener, you will learn about your audience from observing their nonverbal behavior. If you can read closely, you will be able to take note of your audience's hidden clues in writing. These observations can help you understand your audience and thus, be able to persuade them effectively.

1. Cultivate listening skills.

Being perceived as a good listener is as important as being known as an effective speaker or writer. Listening is a crucial skill, and it's complicated by the fact that listening habits vary from individual to individual and culture to culture. One way to determine whether you are a good listener is to notice how often you interrupt others. People who interrupt often tend to not listen very well, although a competitive environment can generate a habit of interruptions. Communication expert Mary Munter notes that "business people spend 45 to 63 percent of their time listening, yet as much as 75 percent of what gets said is ignored, misunderstood, or forgotten." These numbers indicate that listening is a difficult skill, but unfortunately, it's seldom taught in the classroom or elsewhere.

Most people are not aware of the skills involved in effective listening, although some researchers now suggest that our growing dependence on oral information, such as from television and other oral media, is increasing our ability to listen and remember what we've heard.

In general, listening is a difficult process for several reasons. Simply hearing is not the same as listening; the hearer does not register or remember everything that is said. Most people cannot pay attention to a single topic for long periods. They tend to expect what they are familiar with and not "hear" the unfamiliar. Finally, listening tends to shut down when emotions are high and/or when the competition to be heard is strong.

Fortunately, however, listening skills can be learned. A good listener will be able to hear both verbal and nonverbal cues in messages; and although listening is most challenged in competitive environments, it is there that listening can be most useful. The following guidelines show effective and ineffective listening strategies:

Effective listeners do the following:

- *Stay quiet and let silences happen.* Particularly in Western cultures, silences are uncomfortable, and many people rush to fill them with words, often making statements or concessions that they later regret. Silences can help you understand the information you have heard.

- *Tune out distractions.* If you can focus on the speaker alone, you will not only better understand what is being said, but you will also be perceived as being engaged in the topic; this will create a positive atmosphere.

- *Hear key ideas and facts.* If you can concentrate well enough, you will be able to organize and remember important points as the speaker proceeds, which will help you to reach appropriate conclusions and come up with relevant questions.

- *Distinguish between position statements and reasons and reasons and evidence.* Careful listening can help you to identify the various parts of a speaker's message, finding both weaknesses and strengths.

- *Stay open-minded until speaker is finished.* Although this is often difficult when you do not agree with the speaker's message, your challenges will be more effective if you appear to have listened carefully to the entire message.

- *Take notes that are brief but on point.* Jotting down key points helps you to remember the substance of the message and shows the speaker that you are taking the message seriously.

- *Pay attention to verbal and nonverbal cues.* Noticing a speaker's word choices, and sometimes sentence constructions, can give you clues about the speaker's attitude toward the topic. Observing nonverbal behavior can tell you about speaker attitudes toward the topic as well as attitudes toward you as the audience.

- *Show interest by eye contact and other facial expressions.* Focus on the speaker, but do not stare fixedly. Avoid looking away for a long period of time. Eye contact is cultural, so be aware of any cultural conventions that would change your usual habits.

Ineffective listeners often do the following:

- *Lack self-confidence.* A person who lacks confidence is easily challenged by what others say, leading to fear of what may happen. This kind of person often holds the floor and talks too much, depriving others of the chance to contribute.

- *Think ahead while others speak.* This is a habit common to many, often caused by environments where it is difficult to be heard. Highly competitive situations where you must interrupt to be able to speak and then talk fast before you, in turn, are interrupted foster poor listening habits.

- *Think they know what is going to be said.* Those who believe they know the message before it is given tend not to listen carefully, and therefore, miss important information.

- *Lack respect for the speaker.* Listeners who do not respect or have confidence in the speaker may not listen at all to the message, or may only listen superficially.

2. Put your listening skills to work.

If you have learned to be a good listener, you will be able to gain understanding of your audience by observing their nonverbal behavior. Nonverbal cues provide a rich source of additional information to what is actually being said. Be especially aware when the nonverbal language is at odds with the words in both oral and written communication. This lack of consistency can suggest underlying conflicts regarding the message. Nonverbal behavior includes: (1) vocal characteristics, (2) facial expression, (3) gestures, and (4) posture. These characteristics are influenced by a speaker's background and natural tendencies; nevertheless, you can gain important information by noticing the following:

Vocal characteristics

- *Tone:* A speaker's attitude toward the topic is clearly communicated if the tone is angry, chastising, sarcastic, conciliatory, and so on. Even if a speaker tries to control the tone, emotion often comes through clearly.

- *Pitch:* A high or low pitch is usually natural to each speaker. However, if a speaker shows a pitch that is not usual, strong emotion is often the reason. For example, a person who has a naturally low voice but who is speaking at a high pitch may be showing fear or nervousness about the situation.

- *Rate of speaking:* A person's normal rate of speaking is usually developed over time and depends on experience. However, like pitch, if a speaker is talking at a rate that is not usual, the reason is often strong emotion.

Facial expression

- *Positive:* lots of eye contact, smiling, leaning head sideways, touching face, facial expressions of interest. For example, the person who smiles at you when you approach is showing a receptive attitude. Likewise, a person listening to you who lightly touches his or her face and is looking at you directly is showing interest in what you are saying.

- *Negative:* little eye contact, squinted eyes, looking at the other person sideways, tense facial expression, hand covering mouth. In Western societies, lack of eye contact is one of the clearest signs of a lack of interest in or agreement with what is being said.

Gestures

- *Positive:* open arms and palms, hands relaxed, putting hands to chest, hand resting outward toward speaker/listener, touching audience.
- *Negative:* arms crossed, hands on hips, hands behind back, hands held tensely in front, gripping arms, hand over mouth, making fists.

Posture

- *Positive:* sitting forward toward audience, sitting toward front of chair, leaning forward, relaxed body, loosening tie or removing jacket, weight equally distributed on both feet, uncrossed legs (if sitting).
- *Negative:* leaning away from audience, buttoning coat or pulling coat together in front, fidgeting, turning body sideways, pointing legs and feet away from audience, crossing legs or ankles (if sitting).

3. Learn to read carefully.

If you want to learn about your audience for future communication, reading what that person has written is a good way to do it. Hints of a hidden subtext in written messages can be both subtle and obvious, but you can receive good information about a writer from noticing several characteristics. One thing to note before discussing written cues is that one way to communicate a negative message is the use of silence. Not answering a message right away can communicate a number of things, including disagreement or lack of interest.

A number of written characteristics provide extra information about the writer's mood and opinions. (1) *Tone,* for example, is often communicated by the use of punctuation. An exclamation mark adds emotion to a declarative or imperative sentence. A question mark can be negative if the context of the sentence is confrontational. (2) *Organization* can also have an impact on the tone of your written message. A message with the main point in the first sentence is often more aggressive than one in which the main point comes after other information. Whether or not this is negative depends on the context of the message. (3) *Focus* is a third factor to consider. A person who usually writes brief messages directly to the point may be showing ambivalence about the topic if his or her message is long and rambling. Alternatively, a person who habitually writes long messages with lots of digressions may be using the writing process to reach a conclusion or decision. In this case, recognizing the stage of the writer's thoughts about the issue can provide an opportunity for influencing the outcome. (4) *Style:* Finally, the overall style of a message can be informative about hidden subtexts. If the writer's style is dramatically different from his or her usual style, it may be that the topic has generated an emotional reaction. For example, an angry writer may write in an atypical way, using long sentences and/or negative words and phrases that do less to achieve objectives than to indicate how the writer is feeling at the moment.

4. Put your reading skills to work.

Two major aspects of writing can provide clues to additional meaning in messages. They are sentence construction and word choice.

Sentence construction choices: When trying to persuade, both writers and speakers construct phrases and sentences to receive the reaction they desire; many times these choices are unconscious. However, you can often "read" the subtext by noticing the kinds of constructions favored in the message, including complex and passive choices.

- *Complex versus simple:* Unsurprisingly, research shows that a simple message is easier to remember than a complex one. However, studies also show that attitudes change less when the points are articulated in complex sentences than they do when the sentences are simpler. According to this research, strong points are more persuasive if they are also communicated in simple sentences; weak points were less effective in both simple and complex constructions. In addition, complex sentence constructions sometimes hide or confuse major points being made. Obviously, sometimes people write messages with lots of complex sentences because of circumstances, complexity of the information, or personal writing style. However, a message comprised of predominantly complex sentences is worth checking for weak points and other hidden clues.

- *Passive versus active:* A construction is active when the subject performs the action that the verb expresses. A construction is passive when the subject benefits from or receives the action the verb expresses. Three characteristics of the passive are (1) the subject does not do the acting; (2) the verb consists of two or more words, one of which is some form of "to be"; (3) the word "by" is expressed or implied. If you read a message with many passive constructions, you should consider why the writer has made this choice. Using a passive construction can distance the communicator from the audience, is less personal, less concise, and less emphatic. It can suggest a lack of accountability. On the other hand, passive constructions are useful for avoiding personal or blunt accusations or commands, when the writer wants to stress the object of the action rather than the doer, and when the doer is not important in the sentence. Careful observation of when and how a speaker or writer uses the passive can give you clues about attitude.

Word choices: Writers choices of words can also provide clues to their attitude toward the subject. Lawrence Hosman (as cited in the bibliography, page 97) outlined four areas of word choice that are important: range, vividness, power, and clarity. Word choices also include positive versus negative.

- *Range:* Range refers to the variety of words used in a message. According to Hosman's newest research, a communicator may try to use a variety of vocabulary to increase credibility. This finding challenges the usual textbook guideline to always use simple words, although using a variety of simple words would resolve this disparity. One note on this issue is that some studies have found that people who lie use a greater variety of word choices than those who do not lie. From a reader's perspective, use of extensive vocabulary in a message can, depending on the context and the relationships involved, suggest an attempt to establish credibility or to obscure the meaning.

- *Vividness:* Vivid words can communicate emotion and tone in a message. Words that are considered vivid create an image in the minds of the audience, and typically this means using concrete terms and details. Mostly, though, a writer's use of vivid words can suggest emotion and how involved the writer is in the message.

- *Power:* Power in words refers to intensity, such as "extremely" instead of "very" and "devastating" instead of "difficult." According to Hosman, strong words can contribute to a perceived dynamism in the communicator and increase audience interest and attention. On the other hand, powerful word choices can also suggest an extreme position in the communicator and sometimes suggest incompetence. If you agree with the message's position, your view of powerful words may be positive. If you do not agree, your view may be negative.

- *Clarity:* Most business textbooks advise clarity in all situations, for obvious reasons. If you do not understand a message, you are less likely to do what the writer wants. Most people believe that clarity is critical to success. If you're reading a message that is ambiguous, ask yourself why the writer might choose to be unclear. Writers may choose ambiguity over clarity: (1) when they want to build consensus on a general issue, such as a policy statement, and they need broad agreement before addressing individual issues, and (2) when they have strong opinions opposed to your own, and as in the first instance, they need only overall agreement to move forward.

- *Positive versus negative:* Hosman suggests that word choice can communicate either a positive or a negative tone. A reader can sense confrontation with such phrases as "You failed to read the directions," and a condescending attitude in examples such as "It should be obvious that . . . " or "You must realize that . . . " In addition, words that emphasize problems or what cannot be done, such as "unfortunate, misinterpret, mistake," or "fail," cast a gloomy shadow over a message. This negativity may be desirable in some circumstances. If a writer is using negative language, ask yourself why. Negative language can reveal a writer's outlook on the topic and on the readers of the message.

Cultivating your listening skills and learning how to read a message carefully can help you answer important questions about your audience for both present and future communication.

CHECKLIST: ANALYZING YOUR AUDIENCE

Analyze your audience

Who are they?
✓ Who are they (primary, secondary, and others)?
✓ What do they know about the subject?
✓ What is their opinion of your position?
✓ What is their preferred channel?
✓ What are their constraints?

What is their personality type?
✓ Creator
✓ Fact-finder
✓ Analyst
✓ Judge

Approaches to consider and use

Cultivate listening skills, including observance of nonverbal behavior.

Cultivate and use reading skills, including sentence construction and word choices.

CHAPTER IV OUTLINE

I. Audience motivation techniques
  1. General motivational strategies
  2. Specific motivational appeals

II. Credibility enhancement techniques
  1. Personal credibility
  2. Organizational credibility

CHAPTER IV

Motivate Your Audience

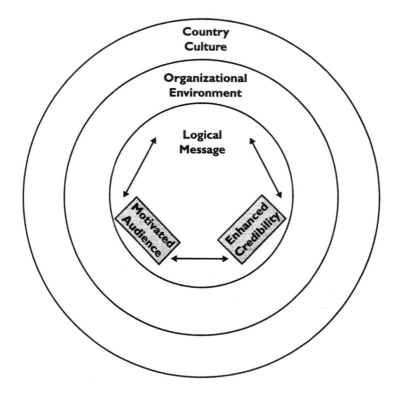

Once you have analyzed your audience, think about what you can do to motivate them and enhance your credibility.

I. AUDIENCE MOTIVATION TECHNIQUES

To motivate your audience, choose from among the following:
(1) general motivational strategies and (2) specific motivational appeals.

1. General motivational strategies

General motivational strategies include soft sell versus hard sell and
strategies based on personality type.

Soft sell or hard sell: One set of strategic choices has to do with
soft sell versus hard sell. Either strategy may be used with anyone in
the organizational hierarchy. Although it may seem intuitive that the
soft sell would be used for superiors, at times a hard sell strategy will
be most persuasive. Consider the request to provide a lunchroom for
staff, and the argument includes the signatures of all staff members.
A superior, depending on his or her personality, might find the out-
numbering tactic compelling.

SOFT SELL VERSUS HARD SELL STRATEGIES	
Soft Sell Strategies	**Hard Sell Strategies**
Logical appeals: Reasons supported by factual evidence	*Barter:* Focusing on audience benefits, exchange of favors, or future advantages for audience
Emotional appeals: Reasons that touch emotions, inspire enthusiasm, and generate feelings of empowerment	*Outnumbering:* Convincing others to join in position and suggesting mass agreement as a reason for persuasion
Advice: Seeking participation indecisions regarding issue by asking for advice and by willingness to compromise depending on audience needs	*Pressure:* Using demands, threats, and constant attention; focusing on details and monitoring each step closely
Praise: Using flattery and compliments to generate positive feelings and increase audience self-confidence	*Rank:* Suggesting agreement because of authority of manager; showing consistency with organizational policies

Strategies based on personality: A second option to consider has to do with basing your strategy on your audience personality, as explained in the following table:

STRATEGIES BASED ON PERSONALITY TYPE		
Role and needs	**Communication implications**	**Try these strategies**
Creator Creates commonality Inspires to greater purpose	**Oral:** Enthusiastic; talks a lot and sometimes fast; interrupts; likes broad issues more than detail **Written:** Likes charts and graphs; less interested in format and more in ideas; likes the unusual	**Soft tactics:** Emotional appeals, praise, and advice
Fact-Finder Manages details	**Oral:** Uses calm, neutral tone; is organized; likes lots of facts and figures **Written:** Needs clarity, facts/evidence; wants precise word choices	**Soft tactics:** Logical appeals **Hard tactics:** Barter (focusing on benefits)
Analyst Promotes agreement	**Oral:** Likes well-organized information, with issues well separated and discussed **Written:** Needs organization, linear reasoning, and supporting data	**Soft tactics:** Logical appeals, advice **Hard tactics:** Barter, pressure, and rank (needs to create agreement any way possible)
Judge Encourages performance Promotes objectives	**Oral:** Likes careful word choices and discussion of advantages and disadvantages **Written:** Tone and status important, and presentation of alternatives to evaluate	**Soft tactics:** Logical appeals **Hard tactics:** Barter, outnumbering

2. Specific motivational appeals

After you have considered your overall strategies, think about specific appeals that will be effective for your audience and for the issue at hand. Consider the following appeals:

Logical (focus on provable facts):

- *What they are:* Logical appeals consist of numbers, statistics, and expert testimony. In Western forms of persuasion, logical appeals can "prove" your point.

- *When to use them:* Use logical appeals when you have an audience whose responsibilities include an organization's financial concerns or who is known to prefer numbers and facts. Use them also when financial matters and the bottom line are important in the situation.

- *Examples:*
  1. Costs to reconfigure the current lunchroom into an IS center will be over $100,000. Costs to use the two offices on the second floor is estimated at $68,000.
  2. This reconfiguration of our manufacturing system will reduce ramp-up time by 50 percentage.

Emotional (focus on feelings):

- *What they are:* Emotional appeals not only touch on the emotions of the audience but also suggest intangible benefits to the person or organization.

- *When to use them:* Use emotional appeals when the situation is not strictly a financial issue and when the happiness and well-being of the audience is part of the situation. Use them also when the rightness of your point of view is not obvious and others may disagree with you. Finally, use these appeals to suggest an intangible benefit in terms of reputation or status.

- *Examples:*
  1. Our secretaries are already upset about not receiving raises this year and being asked to park in the farthest lot; to ask them to give up their lunchroom could cause an overt rebellion.
  2. This reconfiguration will add to XYZ's reputation as a leader in next-generation manufacturing systems.

Ethical (focus on right and wrong):

- *What they are:* Ethical appeals relate to a person's sense of right and wrong. As such, they are culturally driven and are almost always reflective of a community rather than an individual belief. In addition, ethical appeals are effective only when the values they are based on are shared by both communicator and audience.
- *When to use them:* Decisions involving moral issues are appropriate for ethical appeals, and these may or may not involve legal issues. Although sometimes they intersect, the law and ethical concerns are not exactly the same, and the law does not cover all ethical behavior.
- *Examples:*
  1. We felt that the right thing to do was to revise our benefits package because of the new regulations regarding 401Ks.
  2. Our secretaries cannot afford to eat lunch out every day, and the current lunchroom provides them with a place to get away and relax while they eat.

Positive (focus on audience rewards):

- *What they are:* Positive appeals simply state the benefits of adopting the point presented. These benefits can be concrete or abstract.
- *Examples:*
  1. Maintaining the current lunchroom will have the benefit of demonstrating to our secretaries that we do care about their needs.
  2. This reconfiguration will allow for an immediate response to market demands.

Negative (focus on audience threats):

- *What they are:* Negative appeals remind an audience of the bad things that can happen if the current recommendation is not taken.
- *Examples:*
  1. One secretary has already resigned, and others may quit if we eliminate their lunchroom.
  2. This reconfiguration will prevent the company from falling behind in market demands.

II. CREDIBILITY ENHANCEMENT TECHNIQUES

Another way to motivate your audience has to do with enhancing your credibility—based on your audience's perception of you, their belief, confidence, and faith in you, on both a personal and organizational level. In fact, credibility is one of the most important factors in persuading others and maintaining influence both within and outside your organization. Building credibility and influence takes time and patience; you need to know what both personal and organizational credibility are and how you can develop them.

1. Personal credibility

Personal credibility is based on your audience's perception of you personally.

What it is: The major components of personal credibility are:

- *Integrity:* the sense of having values and being willing to adhere to them both publicly and privately
- *Honesty:* being willing to tell the truth so that others trust what you say; this includes telling the truth tactfully and does not imply that truth-telling must always be painful
- *Sincerity:* concern and interest in audience needs and a genuine desire for others' well-being
- *Fairness:* the sense of understanding all sides of an issue and alertness to justice for all parties involved in a situation
- *Openness:* being able and willing to consider diverse points of view; the absence of a perceived hidden agenda

Personal credibility is especially important for persuading people in flatter, more decentralized organizations. However, personal credibility is often important even in traditional, hierarchical organizations. For example, new managers of a company in trouble are constantly judged by the decisions they make. Once the company is doing well, their credibility will increase because they have established themselves as competent leaders.

Although personal credibility is influenced by the power structures in organizations, there are ways to develop your personal credibility that can help you in whatever position you hold.

How you can develop it: First, you need to be patient; developing credibility occurs step-by-step and situation-by-situation over time. In the meantime, you will be asked to persuade others in a variety of situations regardless of your position and how well or poorly others view you. To be persuasive with those within and outside your organization, consider the following suggestions:

- *Respect your audience.* Understand that your audience may not know everything you know about the situation, but they are capable of following a line of reasoning; your audience may need to know the basis of your decision or position in order to be comfortable with it.

- *Study their needs.* As covered in the previous chapter, know who your audiences are and what their concerns are. Try to use referent power to generate common objectives and expert power when possible. This includes, at times, naming your sources of information.

- *Don't make assumptions.* Just because you hold a position of power in your organization, you can't assume that you are credible to all your potential audiences. When you are in doubt about your credibility in a situation, try to support your position with reasons and evidence, as suggested in Chapter I.

2. Organizational credibility

Organizational credibility, on the other hand, is based on your power derived from the organization in which you work. Personal credibility and organizational credibility can overlap, and organizational credibility is often dependent on circumstances.

What it is: Studies by French, Raven, Wheeless, Barraclough, and Stewart (all cited in the bibliography) provide a framework for analyzing organizational credibility, as summarized in the following table:

ORGANIZATIONAL CREDIBILITY		
Legitimate power based on position in organization	**Referent power** based on audience's values, concerns	**Expert power** based on your expertise
• Refers to a relatively high corporate status	• Emphasizes audience values and concerns	• Must be seen as relevant and applicable in situation
• Often includes ability to reward or punish subordinates	• Makes connections between their values and yours	• Must be recognized by audience (may take time to establish)
• Most effective in a traditional, hierarchical organization	• Most effective in a less hierarchical organization or with peers or colleagues	• Useful in all types of organizations

How you can use it:

- *Legitimate power:* Legitimate power is especially useful for people who work in a hierarchical organization. For example, you could say, as CEO (or Vice President or your supervisor), I have decided to change our method of trip reimbursements to better reflect overall strategic goals.
- *Referent power:* Referent power is most effective in less hierarchical organizations or with peers or colleagues. For example, you could say, we have all had problems with the current method of travel reimbursements (list the problems). Then, explain how the new system will solve all of those problems.

- *Expert power:* Expert power is useful in all organizations. For example, you could explain how you came up with the new travel reimbursement system using your expertise to do so.

By using the techniques described in this chapter, you will become more persuasive by motivating your audience and enhancing your own credibility.

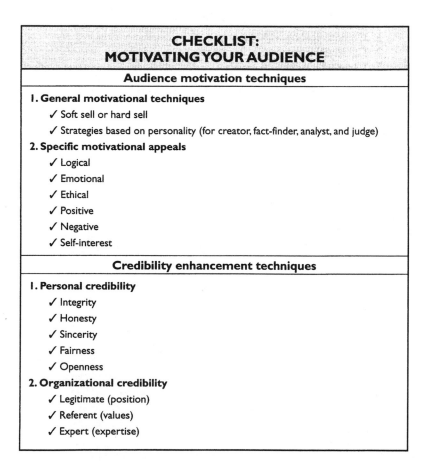

CHECKLIST: MOTIVATING YOUR AUDIENCE

Audience motivation techniques

1. General motivational techniques
- ✓ Soft sell or hard sell
- ✓ Strategies based on personality (for creator, fact-finder, analyst, and judge)

2. Specific motivational appeals
- ✓ Logical
- ✓ Emotional
- ✓ Ethical
- ✓ Positive
- ✓ Negative
- ✓ Self-interest

Credibility enhancement techniques

1. Personal credibility
- ✓ Integrity
- ✓ Honesty
- ✓ Sincerity
- ✓ Fairness
- ✓ Openness

2. Organizational credibility
- ✓ Legitimate (position)
- ✓ Referent (values)
- ✓ Expert (expertise)

CHAPTER V OUTLINE

I. Analyze the organizational environment
   1. Thick or flat?
   2. Centralized or decentralized?
   3. Functional, product, or matrix?
   4. Stable or flexible?
   5. Preferred message channels

II. Analyze your organizational position
   1. Communicating with superiors
   2. Communicating with subordinates
   3. Communicating with equals

CHAPTER V

Study the Organization

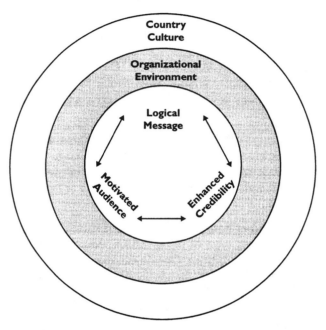

To persuade effectively, you not only have to be able to construct a logical argument, motivate your audience, and enhance your credibility, you should also keep in mind the organization in which you are communicating. The organization will influence, and sometimes control, the process and conventions of how things get done. Being able to recognize and fulfill these expectations can help you become more persuasive. This chapter includes strategies on how to determine what the organizational environment is like and how you fit into it.

I. ANALYZE THE ORGANIZATIONAL ENVIRONMENT

To understand the culture of the organization in which you work or with which you will be dealing, you may have formal training, informal mentoring, or do some detective work on your own. To help you figure out how things get done, consider the following organizational characteristics.

1. Thick or flat?

Start by studying an organizational chart. If it's complex, it will look "thick." If it's relatively simple, it will look "flat." The chart can show you how many levels of hierarchy exist and who reports to whom.

Thick: The more levels of reporting relationships, the thicker the structure. This kind of structure is common in large organizations with many specialized tasks. The reason for specialization is that the fewer tasks someone must perform, the better his or her performance will be.

Flat: On the other hand, a flatter organization does not have as many layers. In this type of organization, employees may have a wide range of responsibilities. One objective of a "flat" organization is to help management make better decisions by putting them closer to the problems.

Communication implications: Knowing whether the organization is thick or flat can show you:

- *The reporting relationships:* Since it's important to find out who the decision makers in the organization are, the organizational chart will show not only the hierarchy, but also the people who have or do not have the power to make the final decisions. In a thick organizational structure, the lower the level, the less responsibility the employee has. Also, a dotted line on a chart will indicate an advisory position rather than a decision-making one. In most cases, your challenge will be to make sure your message reaches those who can make the decision to do what you want.

- *The division of labor:* If there are many specialized jobs, you can note who is responsible for what, and this knowledge will allow you to get needed information when necessary and decide whom to include when you have to communicate a message. A thicker organization with many specialized tasks will be harder to penetrate than one that is flatter, with fewer people doing more tasks. Although a flatter organization will often provide more opportunity for initiative, in a thicker organization you can persuade by just getting the decision maker to agree.

2. Centralized or decentralized?

An organizational chart is a first step toward understanding the organizational culture, but it doesn't tell you everything. It may not indicate a person's actual range of control, for example, or the importance of the responsibilities. In addition to the organizational chart, you should consider a closely related aspect: centralization.

Centralized: Centralization refers to the degree to which a few people at the top of the organizational structure hold most of the decision-making power. In a highly centralized organization, major decisions are made by those at the top, thus limiting the responsibility of those doing routine jobs.

Decentralized: A decentralized organization, on the other hand, has more people at more levels making major decisions, allowing decisions to be made by those closest to the problems.

Communication implications: Communication tends to be more straightforward in a centralized structure because you know exactly who the decision makers are and what levels you need to pass through to reach them. You are always aware that decisions are made by those with a strategic view of the company and the situation. On the other hand, communication tends to be freer in a less centralized organization, but the decision makers are often less visible, and there can be hidden constituencies who can affect the outcome of your communication. In this case, you may need to gather additional information in order to identify the right person for your message.

3. Functional, product, or matrix?

Another way to determine how to communicate across an organization is to consider how departments are set up. Are they organized by function, product, or both (matrix)?

Functional: In this common organizational structure, employees who perform similar functions are in the same department, such as production, sales, accounting, and so on. To be persuasive in this kind of organization, you need to:

- Be aware that communicating across functional areas can be difficult.
- Be able to communicate information clearly and demonstrate relevance to your audience.
- Realize that each functional area has a somewhat narrow view of each issue.
- Create relationships across areas.

Product: Also known as "project" structure, this approach is often used by large organizations that have many types of products or businesses. Each self-contained division has functional staff (in production, sales, accounting, etc.) to handle everything to do with the product. In this kind of organization, you need to:

- Find out if managers have created an open environment with a free flow of communication.
- Realize that communicating across divisions can be very difficult.
- Take extra care in learning about your audience if you are dealing with issues and objectives that require another division's response.

Matrix: This kind of organizational structure combines both function and product. Most people have two bosses, one from the functional area and another from the product or project area. This structure is often ideal for organizations that need to be flexible or whose outside environment is unstable. In a matrix organization, you should:

- Expect some frustration in dealing with multiple bosses.
- Realize that communicating is even more important in this situation because of the need for agreement by more than one supervisor.
- Persist in discussing your issues because this can sometimes enhance communication and therefore help achieve objectives.

4. Stable or flexible?

Some organizations change their structure based on the environment. For example, organizations in the auto and the food service industries are relatively stable and can operate with a more hierarchical and rule-based structure. On the other hand, organizations in high-technology industries change rapidly, and the organizational structure must be able to adjust quickly. These descriptions are the extremes. Organizations can be anywhere on the scale of stable to flexible.

Stable: An organization will often have a stable structure if the industry presents few or no unexpected changes, or if changes only occur slowly over time. This structure provides for highly specialized employees and departments and is most often organized strictly with standardized policies that cover most processes, including communication. Most decisions in this model are made at the top. In terms of communication, ways and means are spelled out clearly, offering established procedures that make it easy to identify how and whom to contact for any issue. If the organization operates in a stable environment, you should:

- Learn quickly the established conventions and procedures for communicating.
- Follow the established procedures. A classic example of a mistake in a stable, hierarchical organization is to "go over the head" of a superior in an attempt to resolve an issue.

Flexible: An organization in a more unstable environment may have a flexible structure. In this kind of organization, there are fewer specialists and more generalists, and much freedom throughout the organization for decision-making and risk-taking initiatives. In this type of structure decisions are made throughout the organization and not by a few people at the top. The structure is flat in terms of hierarchy. To persuade effectively in a flexible environment, you should:

- Realize you may be able to communicate with almost anyone in the organization because there are fewer established policies.
- Take care to determine the right audience for your message since the decision maker may not be easy to identify and may vary from situation to situation.

5. Preferred message channels

Your ability to persuade within an organization is also influenced by the preferred message channels established by either policy or habit. Think about—or find out about—the usual way people communicate. For example, sometimes a quick word in passing can get more results than a formal written memorandum.

Many people believe that executives prefer face-to-face communication. Some do, but not all, and preferences depend on many factors, including what the message is and who is sending it. Consider the following factors when deciding on your message channel:

Face-to-face

- Use this channel when (1) the message is urgent, (2) there are no face-saving issues, or (3) if you have an established relationship with your audience.
- Consider another channel when there are issues of face in the situation, that is, your audience might lose status or credibility because of your message.

Telephone/voicemail

- Use this channel when (1) you can't present your message in person, but it is urgent, or (2) you want the distance the telephone or voicemail gives you.

Email

- Use this channel when (1) your message is routine but somewhat urgent, (2) you want to give your audience time to understand your message, think about it, and respond or not, or (3) you want to save face in a message that might be critical or threatening.
- Consider another channel when your message is sensitive and/or personal.

Memos, letters, reports

- Use this message channel when (1) you have a lot of information to communicate, (2) your audience may need to read your message carefully to understand, or (3) you want documentation for future reference.
- Consider another channel when your message is sensitive and nonroutine.

II. ANALYZE YOUR ORGANIZATIONAL POSITION

Once you have analyzed the organization, consider your own position relative to that of your audience. Within your organization, are you superior to, equal to, or subordinate to your audience? With an outside organization, are you the "buyer," the "seller," or a peer? To make the best communication choices in view of your position to your audience, consider the following strategies.

1. Communicating with superiors

In general, if you are communicating with a superior, your best strategy is to (1) follow the established lines of communication, if they exist and (2) adopt the kind of channel and style favored by your audience. Your strategy should vary depending on whether the organization has a strong or weak hierarchy and whether your audience is internal or external.

Strong hierarchy: In a strong hierarchical organization, you should:

- Use your audience's preferred channel, even if you have a close relationship.
- Make sure you follow established lines of communication.
- Appeal to referent power (see page 58) if you are speaking for others or expert power if you have special knowledge of the issue.

Weak hierarchy: In a weak hierarchical organization, you should:

- Take care to identify the right person with whom to communicate. Remember that decision-making in flatter organizations can shift from one person to another depending on the situation.
- Make special efforts to tailor your message to what you know about your audience's attitudes, if you know them, because your relative organizational status may be unclear.
- Maintain appropriate formality and objectivity if you do not know your audience well. Weak hierarchical organizations can tempt you to assume informality when it isn't appropriate.
- Try to use referent power when possible and expert power if it applies in your case.

2. Communicating with subordinates

Superiors in an organization often assume that their position alone ("legitimate power," as discussed on page 58) is enough to persuade their employees to comply with their decisions. In strong hierarchical organizations, the power of position can be sufficient. However, in flatter organizations, subordinates can become resentful in the face of overt legitimate power. The following strategies can help you deal with subordinates in strong and weak hierarchical organizations.

Strong hierarchy: In a strong hierarchical organization, you should:

- Feel free to appeal to legitimate power and control the message channel and communication style.
- Make sure your message is delivered by the right person. A meat-packing plant once experienced riots when the general manager of the plant sent the human resources director to announce extensive layoffs. In a strong hierarchical organization, the more important the message, the higher in the hierarchy the person who gives it should be.

Weak hierarchy: In a weaker hierarchical organization, you should:

- Be respectful of them personally and of their point of view.
- Identify their concerns about the issue.
- Provide enough reasons and evidence for your decision. Your subordinates must comply with your decision, and if they have not been included in the process, they may not know the reasoning that led to it or the benefits they will have as a result.
- Appeal to referent power based on their values and concerns.
- Try to avoid appealing to legitimate power since your position may not command automatic respect and obedience.

3. Communicating with equals

Communicating with equals depends almost entirely on two things: (1) your reputation in the organization and (2) your relationship with your audience. You can establish your reputation by following the guidelines for building credibility (pages 56–59). Your relationship to your audience is more sensitive and will take careful thought and planning, especially if the issue is important to you. Two challenges in particular are present when dealing with equals.

Recognizing your equals: Knowing who your equals are is equally difficult in strong and weak hierarchical organizations. Remember the following:

- Don't assume your status is superior to those in another department or division. Even in an organization with a strong, clear hierarchy, communicating across departments or divisions can be frustrating. A common mistake is for a person to speak to someone in another part of the organization from a position of superiority when the relative status is not clear.

- Remember that status is often ambiguous in less hierarchical organizations and those making decisions can change with the situation.

Competing priorities: The other challenge in dealing with equals is that often the issues have competing considerations from one section of the organization to another. Priorities in the accounting department are usually different from the priorities in the sales department, and to persuade in this case means creating agreement between opposing positions. Try to do the following:

- Develop a close relationship with your audience, especially if you will be working with this person on a regular basis.

- Learn everything you can about the concerns of your audience's department or division. Then plan your message carefully in terms of language, organization, and channel.

Recognizing your status relative to your audience in an organization is only the beginning in your efforts to build up influence and be persuasive over time. Knowing your audience well on a professional and personal level can offer advantages. A well-established relationship generally allows you to be more informal in your communications, regardless of your relative status. For example, a longtime executive secretary can often give advice and opinions to the executive even though the positions are far apart in the organizational structure. On the other hand, you must always take care not to try to capitalize on a personal relationship in the workplace if that is not an accepted business norm. In the United States, personal relationships are generally reserved for outside the workplace. However, this may not be true in other areas of the world—as we will discuss in the following chapter.

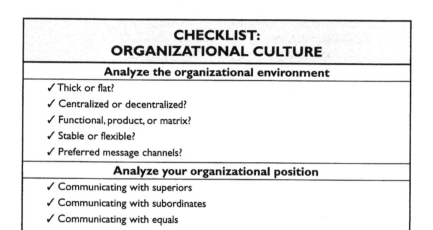

CHECKLIST: ORGANIZATIONAL CULTURE

Analyze the organizational environment

✓ Thick or flat?
✓ Centralized or decentralized?
✓ Functional, product, or matrix?
✓ Stable or flexible?
✓ Preferred message channels?

Analyze your organizational position

✓ Communicating with superiors
✓ Communicating with subordinates
✓ Communicating with equals

CHAPTER VI OUTLINE

I. Social framework: high or low context?
1. High context cultures
2. Low context cultures

II. Time: linear, flexible, or cyclical?
1. Linear view
2. Flexible view
3. Cyclical view

III. Society: individual or collectivist?
1. Individualist cultures
2. Collectivist cultures

IV. Employees: free agents or groups?
1. Free agent cultures
2. Group-oriented cultures

V. Authority: democratic or authoritarian?
1. Authoritarian cultures
2. Democratic cultures

VI. Silence: comfortable or uncomfortable?
1. Cultures comfortable with silence
2. Cultures uncomfortable with silence

VII. Gender: female or male?
1. Women's communication style
2. Men's communication style

CHAPTER VI

Consider the Culture

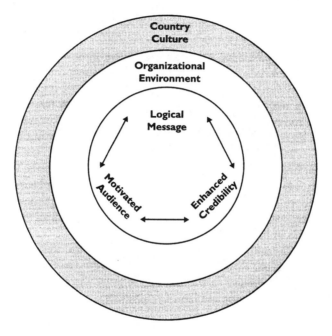

Globalization has led to a dramatic change in the workplace over the past few decades. The United States has become profoundly more heterogeneous due to an increasingly diverse workforce and the need to market products and services in other parts of the world. Even more homogeneous societies such as Japan have been affected by doing business in a globalized economy. Therefore, to be persuasive, you need to take into consideration the culture of the country or region in which you're doing business.

In view of the differences in cultural behavior, being persuasive in your own culture does not guarantee being persuasive in other cultures. For example, if you are an American with traditional roots in western European culture or you have lived in the United States for many years, you may consider yourself to be informal and friendly. You are probably generally direct in your communication style, and you may be dynamic and enthusiastic in your work. These are considered positive traits by most Americans, and they are effective in many situations in the workplace. However, these same traits may be viewed differently by people from other cultures: the friendliness and informality may be seen as too familiar; the direct communication style may seem rude; and the enthusiasm may seem overbearing and even untrustworthy. Therefore, even the most well-meaning businessperson may have problems when dealing with the variety of groups in today's organizations.

To learn to persuade in this multicultural environment, you need to examine cultural differences by considering six factors: (1) social framework (high or low context), (2) view of time, (3) view of society, (4) view of employee, (5) view of authority, and (6) comfort with silence. This chapter ends with a discussion of gender characteristics, an issue that is influenced by the cultural factors mentioned above and is important in its own right.

For more information about the cross-cultural ideas presented in this chapter, see Reynolds and Valentine, *Guide to Cross-Cultural Communication* (listed in the bibliography at the end of this book along with a more complete list of references).

I. SOCIAL FRAMEWORK: HIGH OR LOW CONTEXT?

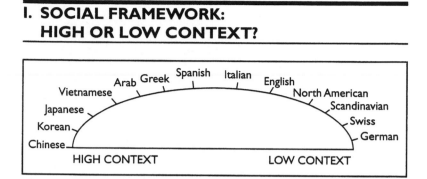

First developed by Edward Hall, the idea of "context" in a culture refers to the amount of commonly assumed information in a society. Differences in the amount of understood knowledge can have an important impact on how your persuasive message is received. A "high context culture" features more implicit communication (based on common values and background). A "low context culture," on the other hand, features more explicit communication (based on the need for clarity in a heterogeneous environment).

1. High context cultures

In a high context culture, much of the text of a message may not be spoken or written, but rather understood within the value system of the group and/or communicated nonverbally.

Characteristics: People in high context cultures . . .

- See work in the context of relationships
- Often prefer indirect organization for messages
- Make decisions by consensus
- Value nonverbal communication
- Accept silence as part of communicating
- Emphasize the overall picture rather than details
- Use abstract or figurative language
- Follow rules sometimes, depending on circumstances

Communication implications: To be more persuasive in high context cultures . . .

- *Establish relationships first.* Don't worry about getting to the point until later. Be more indirect until you know more about your audience. Knowing your audience includes acknowledging their position in the hierarchy and their concerns, finding common ground between you, and fostering friendship. Only when you have established a friendly relationship will you be able to do business. Therefore, patience is important.

- *Take notice of nonverbal communication and learn to be comfortable with silence.* People in high context cultures communicate much of their messages nonverbally through body language, eye contact, and silence. Learning to read these cues will help you interpret your audience's message and respond effectively.

- *Understand the value of oral versus written agreements.* Traditionally, many high context cultures place a greater value on oral agreements than on written ones. Oral agreements are binding in this kind of culture whereas written agreements are not binding, but rather are a starting point for progressing with the issue at hand. If you come from a low context culture and need a written agreement, be sure to come to a firm oral understanding before you insist on a written contract.

- *Focus on the overall picture.* Both written and oral communication should focus on broad issues rather than the details. Allow details to be included as attachments to contracts or other written messages or as follow-up statements to oral messages.

- *Realize that the rules may be changed depending on circumstances.* In a high context culture, rules are understood to be starting points for going forward, and if they are viewed as an impediment, they may be changed. Try to stay flexible when persuading in these circumstances.

2. Low context cultures

People in low context cultures do not "read between the lines" in their messages. They need to have points stated clearly and explicitly to avoid misunderstandings based on the lack of shared values and background. Countries that tend to be low context include United States, Sweden, Norway, Switzerland, and Germany. Within the U.S., the Northeast might also be considered a low context culture compared to the South.

Characteristics: People in low context cultures . . .

- See work as separate from relationships
- Prefer direct structure of messages
- Make decisions individually
- Value verbal communication; may not notice nonverbal signals
- Find silence uncomfortable
- Emphasize details
- Use clear, explicit language
- Follow rules as stated

Communication implications: To be persuasive in low context cultures . . .

- *Be direct and get to the point early.* When you deal with people from low context cultures, remember that the most important matter to them is the issue under discussion. Although some friendly chatting is permissible, your focus should quickly move to the topic under discussion. Personal relationships are not only less important in a low context culture, they may be frowned upon since personal relationships are kept separate from professional relationships.

- *Focus on verbal communication.* Words are crucial in low context cultures. Nonverbal communication, such as body language, may be revealing but is not considered important. Remember that silence is rarely used as a communication strategy; if you stay silent, your audience may fill the silence with words.

- *Understand the importance of written agreements.* Oral agreements are usually not binding. Written agreements, however, are necessary in order to progress with a discussion or a project. These agreements are considered binding and are therefore used for documentation, proof of intent, and a record of the facts.

- *Focus on facts and details.* To be persuasive in low context cultures, provide enough facts and details for your audience to make their own judgments. Figurative and abstract language may not be valued as much as in higher context societies.

- *Realize that the rules must be followed.* Not following the rules and established procedures can prevent agreement on an issue. Even more important, it can undo an agreement even if it has been made.

II. TIME: LINEAR, FLEXIBLE, OR CYCLICAL?

Are people in your culture usually late for meetings? On time? Early? People view time in culturally determined ways, labeled by cross-cultural expert Sana Reynolds as "linear," "flexible," or "cyclical." Keep in mind, however, that people's use of time may be influenced not only by their culture but also by their personalities and their experience with others. For example, multi-tasking has become more evident in the workplace even with businesspeople who take a linear approach to time; relationships become more critical the more global the organization becomes; and deadlines have to be met eventually, even in organizations that view them as flexible.

I. Linear view

People from cultures with a linear view of time—such as western Europe and North America—consider time in distinct segments. A workday begins and ends with clear transitions from one task to the next, one week to the next, and one year to the next.

Characteristics: People in cultures with a linear view of time . . .

- View time as an entity that can be saved, spent, or lost
- Try to complete tasks in some kind of order, finishing one before beginning another
- Make an effort to follow a schedule
- Focus on the task at hand
- Keep work and family and social life separate

Communication implications: To be more persuasive in cultures with a linear view of time . . .

- *Be on time.* Generally, linear cultures value being on time for meetings. This norm is influenced, however, by the organization and by the person who runs the meeting.
- *Expect deadlines to be firm.* Dates you have agreed on with your audience in terms of both interim and final deadlines are generally immovable. To change them, you must renegotiate.
- *Learn to focus on one project or one issue at a time.* Linear project negotiators often want to agree on each issue separately and will discuss each one before moving on to the next.

2. Flexible view

People in cultures with a flexible view of time—such as Arabic countries, Latin American countries, and southern Europeans—generally see time as one long piece that rolls along as the day develops, with one segment of time blending into the next.

Characteristics: People in cultures with a flexible view of time . . .

- View time as an ongoing process that is flexible
- Work on more than one project at a time; are adept at multi-tasking
- Don't worry about a schedule but rather react as the day's events evolve
- Focus on relationships involved in the task rather than the task itself
- Blend work, family, and social life

Communication implications: To be more persuasive in cultures with a flexible view of time . . .

- *Allow more time for appointments.* People from flexible time cultures may arrive at meetings long after the scheduled time. This lateness does not show any lack of respect or commitment. Also, meetings may go longer than anticipated. Both lateness and longer-than-scheduled appointments reflect the flexible time person's custom of reacting as the day's events evolve.
- *Expect deadlines to be flexible.* Deadlines are not firm and can change depending on circumstances. Often, deadlines will not be established at all, and you are expected to understand the timing based on the situation. You should have patience and allow plenty of time to accomplish your objectives.
- *Learn to deal with more than one issue at a time.* This approach can be effective, especially when the issues are interdependent. Again, patience will help you cope with seemingly disorganized discussions.

3. Cyclical view

A third approach to time is the cyclical view. People in cyclical time cultures such as many Native American, Asian, and African cultures see events as recurring in patterns which represent the cycles of life. In order to live in harmony with nature, people in these cultures must understand and adjust to these life cycles.

Characteristics: People in cultures with a cyclical view of time . . .

- View time as circular and repetitive
- Complete tasks over a long period that includes time for reflection
- Focus on the long term in accomplishing tasks and establishing relationships

Communication implications: To be more persuasive in cyclical time cultures . . .

- *Allow time to build relationships.* If a friendly relationship has not been established, you will not be able to go forward with your plans and objectives.
- *Learn to read nonverbal behavior.* Communicating in a cyclical culture depends to a great degree on being able to "read between the lines." You can note the subtext of an interaction by noticing facial expressions and body language.
- *Be on time.* Although organizations within cyclical cultures may vary, lateness may be interpreted as showing disrespect or lack of commitment.

III. SOCIETY: INDIVIDUALIST OR COLLECTIVIST?

Another set of cultural norms has to do with individualism versus collectivism. Both approaches are equally valid even though people from each type of culture tend to be critical of those from the other type.

1. Individualist cultures

Individualist cultures value freedom and independence. Responsibility may reside with a single person who has final decision-making powers. The United States is a strongly individualist culture, and this individualism influences even those who originally come from more collectivist cultures. Other individualist cultures include Scandinavia, Italy, England, France, the United States, Germany, and Switzerland.

Characteristics: People in individualist cultures . . .

- Provide for great personal financial and social rewards (such as prestige)
- Value individual performance and will promote or demote accordingly
- View self-interest as a positive force since it can raise each person's level of performance, thus contributing to the success of the group
- Believe collectivist reliance on teamwork and consensus slows the process

Communication implications: To be more persuasive in individualist cultures . . .

- *Be direct.* Individualist cultures want to get right to the point and not waste time. Although friendly chatting sometimes occurs before serious talks, it is generally brief.
- *Be frank and open about expectations.* Concerns and needs are usually discussed clearly and at or near the beginning of the discussion. In individualist cultures, people view clear expression of expectations as a blueprint to follow in proceeding with the issue.

- *Have all the facts.* Come prepared to make a decision, or at least to move forward with the issue. This means having details and specific plans.
- *Be willing to negotiate with one person.* Individualist societies may send only one person to discuss important projects.

2. Collectivist cultures

Collectivist cultures, on the other hand, value the community as a whole. Individuals within the community are defined by their membership and feel loyalty to the group. Japan and Arabic countries are collectivist; Latin America is generally collectivist, but some Latin American countries, such as Brazil, show many individualist characteristics.

Characteristics: People in collectivist cultures . . .

- Provide for financial and social rewards for the group as a whole
- Value group performance and will reward or penalize the group as a whole
- Value harmony and face-saving strategies
- Believe individualism is selfish and disruptive to the final objective

Communication implications: To be more persuasive in collectivistic cultures . . .

- *Take time to establish relationships.* To be able to move forward with an issue, take the time to get to know your audience. This may mean not getting to the point until later in the discussions.

- *Focus on the overall picture.* Speak and write in broader and less detailed terms. Keep details and specific plans for later in the discussions or for private discussions outside of the major meetings.

- *Send a group for important discussions.* For cultures that value teamwork and consensus-building, choosing only one person to deal with an issue can be a problem, since the group may believe you do not think the matter is important enough for appropriate decision-making. You should also expect them to send several people to deal with you.

IV. EMPLOYEES: FREE AGENTS OR GROUPS?

How does your culture view employees in relation to the organization? Does it consider you a free agent working for an outside entity or as part of a group with a sense of community? In a "free agent culture" (also called a "mechanistic culture"), employees market themselves and work for individual objectives. In contrast, a "group-oriented culture" (also called a "humanistic culture"), fosters a sense of community and achievement of group objectives. Organizations in all cultures can exhibit either of the approaches; at times, both approaches are evident in a single organization.

I. Free agent cultures

Free agent cultures are most common in countries that developed from classical Greek and Roman civilizations such as England, France, Germany, Switzerland, and the Scandinavian, and North American countries.

Characteristics: Free agent cultures view employees as a marketable product who . . .

- Work for wages and benefits
- Move from job to job to improve circumstances
- Can be fired under certain circumstances

Communication implications: To be more persuasive in free agent cultures . . .

- *Appeal to your audience's sense of personal reward in terms of money and recognition.* These rewards can range from security, acceptance, recognition, and approval by others to self-fulfillment needs.

- *Make expectations explicit and words clear.* Include details, clarity in both oral and written messages, and link your expectations to audience benefits.

- *Create a sense of opportunity.* Even if you can't provide individual benefits for your audience, you may be able to persuade by providing opportunities for future individual benefits.

2. Group-oriented cultures

Many of the countries that take a group-oriented view, such as Japan, Latin American countries, and Arabic countries, have developed from Asian and Middle Eastern cultures. However, recent globalization is changing many of the places with a group-oriented view of employees.

Characteristics: Group-oriented cultures view employees as part of a group or community who . . .

- Are partially dependent on connections to others
- Keep the same job for a long time out of loyalty
- Tend not to be fired

Communication implications: To be more persuasive in group-oriented cultures . . .

- *Try to create external harmony.* Suggest benefits for the group or community in terms of harmony and goodwill. Use politeness strategies to avoid confrontation and blame.
- *Focus on the overall picture.* Use words that are less explicit and more abstract. Put details in secondary positions in a document, such as in an attachment. Stress the community value of the point of the message.
- *Emphasize group success.* Focus on group benefits and accomplishments. Suggest future benefits or opportunities for the group.

V. AUTHORITY: DEMOCRATIC
OR AUTHORITARIAN?

In Chapter V, we discussed how the organization often determines the norms concerning authority. However, these norms are also heavily influenced by culture. Intercultural researcher Geert Hofstede's concept of "power distance" (cited on page 97) provides a helpful way to analyze authority. "High power distance" means a lot of distance between those at the top and those at the bottom—"authoritarian" cultures. "Low power distance" means the opposite, less distance between those at the top and the bottom—democratic cultures.

1. Authoritarian cultures

In authoritarian cultures, inequalities are recognized, and the "power distance" is high. Recognizing and respecting status and relationships is important. Those who come from cultures with this view are usually comfortable with hierarchical organizations and can take direction with few problems. Examples of authoritarian cultures include Japan, Latin American countries, and Arabic countries.

Characteristics: People in authoritarian cultures . . .

- Have generally authoritarian values
- Value conformity over personal achievement
- Place more importance on fairness than freedom

Communication implications: To be more persuasive in authoritarian cultures . . .

- *Establish your credibility.* At times, your position alone will generate compliance and/or agreement in your audience. At other times your association with someone of higher rank will help.
- *Use the hierarchy to your advantage.* In high power distance cultures, knowing who the decision makers are will allow you to leverage the organizational structure to help you persuade.

2. Democratic cultures

Democratic, or "low power distance," cultures tend to recognize everyone as equal. Since people in this environment feel equal to everyone else, gaining consensus and listening to many viewpoints are common persuasive strategies. The authority norms here are weak. Low power distance countries include England, Scandinavian countries, and North American countries.

Characteristics: People in democratic cultures . . .

- Value individuality and personal contributions
- Believe everyone is equal even when one position is higher in the hierarchy than the other

Communication implications: To be more persuasive in democratic cultures . . .

- *Don't overestimate your credibility.* Research shows that many people in legitimate power positions assume that their position provides them with credibility. However, their subordinates in a low power distance organization discount this kind of credibility and need evidence and other support in order to "buy in" to the decision.
- *Provide reasoning and evidence for decisions.* The lower the power distance and the more democratic the culture, the more expert power, as well as facts and evidence, you will need to persuade others because they may question every point.

VI. SILENCE: COMFORTABLE
OR UNCOMFORTABLE?

Cultures that are comfortable with silence often use it as a powerful communication strategy. When U.S. companies first started negotiating with the Japanese in the middle of the twentieth century, they often made many unplanned concessions because they were unused to silence. The Americans tended to speak without pauses and expected immediate responses. The Japanese, on the other hand, were comfortable with extensive silences between one group of comments and the next. So when the Americans were met with silence, they continued to talk, and when they finally finished, they often had given up more than they wanted.

1. Cultures comfortable with silence

In some cultures, those who are quiet are thought to be more knowledgeable than those who are more vocal; a Confucian concept states, "Those who speak do not know; those who know do not speak." Countries comfortable with silence are Japan, South Korea, and Scandinavian countries.

Characteristics: People from cultures comfortable with silence . . .

- Try to maintain control of discussion by use of silence
- Believe that what is not said can be important

Communication implications: To be more persuasive in cultures comfortable with silence . . .

- *Rearrange communication priorities.* Don't expect to move through your points in a linear fashion. Learn to tolerate diversions from the topic under discussion.
- *Speak slowly.* This includes allowing more space between one sentence and the next.
- *Accept silence.* In addition to speaking slowly, try to develop the ability to sit quietly for some period without speaking at all.

2. Cultures uncomfortable with silence

People in other cultures find silence disconcerting and uncomfortable. They may continue to talk if others are quiet. Examples include Latin American, western European, and North American countries.

Characteristics: People in cultures uncomfortable with silence . . .

- May fill every gap in conversation with words such as "you know what I mean?" or "uh's" and "um's."
- Try to maintain control over discussion by preventing silences

Communication implications: To be more persuasive in cultures uncomfortable with silence . . .

- *Learn to "keep the floor."* Prepare ahead of time so that you have plenty to say, and make an effort to deliver an entire point before allowing anyone else to speak. This may mean talking faster than is usual for you and not allowing any gaps of silence in your delivery.
- *Expect interruptions.* Learn to accept that others may interrupt at any point for questions about what you are saying or for comments of their own. Interruptions in this kind of culture suggest that the listeners are fully engaged and interested in what you are saying.

VII. GENDER: FEMALE OR MALE?

Communication between men and women is affected by cultural factors. Gender issues are included here as part of the intercultural discussion because women make up a large portion of the workplace in many areas of the world. Even in countries where women traditionally do not seek paid employment, such as Japan, more and more women are entering the workforce. Because relations between women and men are complex, communication in professional contexts offers many challenges.

Much research has been done on the communication differences between men and women. According to researcher Deborah Tannen (cited on page 96), women consider communication to be what holds relationships together by creating connections and a sense of belonging. For men, though, activities hold relationships together, and communication is used to negotiate and maintain position and power. Understanding these differences in communication styles can help both women and men become effective persuaders. In cultures that value directness and aggressiveness, men's communication style can be more effective. In cultures that value relationship and consensus-building, women's style can be more effective.

I. Women's communication style

Women use language and nonverbal communication to create and maintain their relationships. However, these traits sometimes suggest uncertainty and emotion.

Characteristics: Women tend to . . .

- See questions as a way to keep conversation flowing
- Expect new comments to reflect what last speaker said
- View aggressiveness as an attack and as negative and disruptive
- Define topics broadly and shift or expand topic gradually
- Respond to a problem with sympathy and offer reassurance and solidarity
- Use the following linguistic strategies: (1) *Questioning tone:* Women tend to use a questioning tone, even when they are sure of their answers, such as "I think this is a good idea?" or "Don't you think so?" (2) *Justifiers:* Women often provide a reason for everything they

say, such as "the reason I say that is." (3) *Intensive adverbs:* Women are more likely than men to use such phrases as "a *really* good book" or "an *exceptionally* good presentation." (4) *Personal pronouns:* Women are adept at speaking and writing with pronouns, such as "we" and "you," which can personalize the message and create an inclusive atmosphere. (5) *Hedges:* Women have a tendency to weaken their statements with such phrases as "sort of, kind of, perhaps," and other similar constructions.

Communication implications: If you're a man communicating with a woman, bear in mind the following . . .

- *Don't misread.* Be careful not to misread "hedges" or a questioning tone of voice as uncertainty.

- *Avoid anger and other emotional displays.* Avoid male put-downs. Anything that is perceived as aggression will most likely be viewed negatively by a woman you are doing business with. Getting her agreement will be difficult if you have created a hostile environment.

- *Take the time to build relationships and consensus.* Discuss all the relevant issues before making a decision. Many women are more comfortable with a consensus decision than an authoritarian one.

- *Don't be condescending.* Although it is not as common today as it was in the past, some men still try to establish a good relationship with a female counterpart by addressing her with terms of endearment, such as "honey," a practice that is totally unacceptable in the workplace. Take care to address her with her appropriate title and avoid using her first name any sooner than you would with a man.

2. Men's communication style

Men use communication as a way to control a situation. Their language and nonverbal choices are often viewed as dynamic.

Characteristics: Men tend to . . .

- See questions as simply requests for information
- Not require their comments to relate to last speaker's comment
- View aggressiveness as one way to control the conversation
- Define the topic narrowly and shift abruptly
- Respond to a problem by offering advice and trying to provide solutions
- Use the following linguistic strategies: (1) *Avoid questions.* Men are more likely to speak in simple, declarative sentences. (2) *Use commands.* Men often give requests as commands, often without politeness markers. (3) *Use few hedges, adverbs, and personal pronouns.* Men's conversations are more fact or opinion oriented, and they do not feel the need for additional modifiers or pronouns of inclusion. (4) *Interrupt often.* Men often control conversations by interrupting and then keeping the floor by using lots of conjunctions (for example, strings of "and") and other fillers.

Communication implications: If you are a woman communicating with a man, bear in mind the following:

- *Don't misread his certainty.* Just because he sounds sure of something doesn't necessarily mean he feels that way. He may be open to disagreement and discussion.
- *Use a stronger communication style.* This includes avoiding such things as hedging your remarks or making apologies. These kinds of communication patterns may make you sound insecure and uncertain.
- *Be brief.* Many women can provide extensive explanations for their point of view, but you should limit this information to only what is immediately relevant. The shorter the better, in most cases.
- *Hold your ground.* Don't let him interrupt you or overpower you with strong language. Be ready to assert yourself with concise statements of your views.
- *Don't misread his intentions.* He may sound certain even when he isn't. An emphatic tone, sarcasm, and joking put-downs may be part of his communication style with everyone, not just you.

Becoming aware of cultural and gender factors is a starting point for understanding the diverse world in which you work. This, combined with your knowledge of how to construct a message, analyze your audience, enhance your credibility, and work within your organizational culture, will help you succeed in developing influence and persuasive power.

CHECKLIST: CULTURE AND GENDER

✓ Are you working in a high or low context culture?

✓ Does your audience view time in a linear, flexible, or cyclical fashion?

✓ Is the view of society individualist or collectivist? Or does it show traits from both?

✓ Do employees view themselves as free agents or as members of a group?

✓ Is your audience's view of authority democratic or authoritarian?

✓ Is your audience comfortable or uncomfortable with silence?

✓ Does your audience include men, women, or both?

Bibliography

Written for managers

Bettinghaus, Erwin Paul, *Persuasive Communication.* New York: Holt, Rinehart & Winston, 1980.

Cialdini, Robert B., "Harnessing the Power of Persuasion," *Harvard Business Review,* October 2002.

Conger, Jay A., "The Necessary Art of Persuasion," *Harvard Business Review,* May–June, 1998.

Jandt, Fred E., *Intercultural Communication,* 3rd ed. Thousand Oaks, CA: Sage, 2001.

Kenton, Sherron B. and Deborah Valentine, *Crosstalk: Communicating in a Multicultural Workplace.* Upper Saddle River, NJ: Prentice Hall, 1997.

Munter, Mary M., *Guide to Managerial Communication,* 6th ed. Upper Saddle River, NJ: Prentice Hall, 2003.

——— "Cross-Cultural Communication for Managers," *Business Horizons,* May 1993.

Murphy, Herta A., Herbert W. Hildebrandt, and Jane P. Thomas, *Effective Business Communications,* 7th ed. New York: McGraw-Hill, 1997.

Ober, Scot, *Contemporary Business Communication,* 2nd ed. Boston, Toronto: Houghton Mifflin, 1995.

Reynolds, Sana and Deborah Valentine, *Guide to Cross-Cultural Communication.* Upper Saddle River, NJ: Prentice Hall, 2003.

Tannen, Deborah, *Talking From 9 to 5: Women and Men in the Workplace: Language, Sex and Power.* New York: Avon Books, 1994.

Williams, Gary A. and Robert B. Miller, "Change the way you persuade," *Harvard Business Review,* May 2002.

Wright, Arthur F. (ed.), *The Confucian Persuasion.* Stanford, CA: Stanford University Press, 1960.

Written for academics

Berlo, David Kenneth, *The Process of Communication.* New York: Holt, Rinehart & Winston, 1960.

Carpenter, R. H., "The Statistical Profile of Language Behavior with Machiavellian Intent or While Experiencing Caution and Avoiding Self-Incrimination," *Annals of the New York Academy of Sciences,* 606, 1990, 5–17.

Chambliss, M. K. and R. Garner, "Do Adults Change Their Minds after Reading Persuasive Text?" *Written Communication,* 13, no. 3, July 1996, 291–313.

Charles, Mirjaliisa and David Charles, "Sales Negotiations: Bargaining through Tactical Summarie," in *Business English: Research into Practice,* M. Hewings and C. Nickerson, (eds.) London: Longman, 1999.

Clyne, M., "Written Discourse Across Cultures," *Intercultural Communication at Work.* Cambridge, England: Cambridge University Press, 1994.

Crismore, Avon, Raija Markkanen, and S. Margaret Steffensen, "Metadiscourse in Persuasive Writing," *Written Communication,* 10, no.1, January 1993, 39–71.

Crystal, David, *English as a Global Language.* Cambridge: England: Cambridge University Press, 1997.

David, Carol and Margaret Ann Baker, "Rereading Bad News: Compliance-Gaining Features in Management Memos," *Journal of Business Communication,* 31, no. 4, 1994, 267–290.

Dillard, James Price and Michael Pfau, *The Persuasion Handbook.* Thousand Oaks, CA: Sage, 2002.

Dulaney, E. F. Jr., "Changes in Language Behavior as a Function of Veracity," *Human Communication Research,* 1982, 75–82.

French, J. R. P. Jr. and B. Raven, "The Bases of Social Power," in *Studies in Social Power,* D. Cartwright (ed.). Ann Arbor: University of Michigan Press, 1959, 150–167.

Hall, E. T., *Beyond Culture.* Garden City, NY: Anchor, 1976.

Harrington, Anne White, *Selecting, Designing and Using Computer-Generated Visual Aids in Oral and Written Consulting Reports.* Project materials for Multidisciplinary Action Projects, University of Michigan Business School, 1998.

Hart, S. L. and R. E. Quinn, "Roles Executives Play: CEOs, Behavioral Complexity, and Firm Performance," *Human Relations,* 46, 1993, 543–574.

Hinds, John, "Inductive, Deductive, Quasi-inductive: Expository Writing in Japanese, Korean, Chinese, and Thai," in *Coherence in Writing,* Ulla Connor and Ann Johns (eds.). Alexandria, VA: Teachers of English to Speakers of Other Languages, Inc., 1990.

Hofstede, Geert, *Culture's Consequences.* Thousand Oaks, CA: Sage, 2001.

Hosman, Lawrence, "Language and Persuasion," in *The Persuasion Handbook,* James Price Dillard and Michael Pfau (eds.). Thousand Oaks, CA: Sage, 2002.

Katz, Daniel, Robert Louis Kahn, and J. Stacy Adams, *The Study of Organizations.* San Francisco, CA: Jossey-Bass, 1980.

Kipnis, D., S. M. Schmidt, and I. Wilkinson, "Intraorganizational Influence Tactics: Explorations in Getting One's Way," *Journal of Applied Psychology,* 65, August 1980, 440–452.

Lamude, K. G. and J. Scudder, "Relationship of Managerial Work Roles to Tactics Used to Influence Subordinates," *Journal of Business Communication,* 32, no. 2, April 1995, 163–174.

Miller, M. D., "Friendship, Power, and the Language of Compliance-Gaining," *Journal of Language and Social Psychology*, 1, 1982, 111–121.

Rogers, Priscilla and Herbert W. Hildebrandt, "Competing Values Instruments for Analyzing Written and Spoken Management Messages," *Human Resource Management*, Spring 1993, 121–142.

Thomas, Jane, "Contexting Koreans: Does the High/Low Model Work?" *Business Communication Quarterly*, 61, no. 4, December 1998, 9–22.

Wheeless, L. R., R. Barraclough, and R. Stewart, "Compliance-Gaining and Power in Persuasion," in *Communication Yearbook 7*, R. E. Bostrom and B. H. Westley (eds.) Beverly Hills, CA: Sage, 1983, 105–145.

Yukl, Gary and Cecilia M. Falbe, "Influence Tactics and Objectives in Upward, Downward, and Lateral Influence Attempts," *Journal of Applied Psychology*, 75, no. 2, 1990, 132–140.

Index